CALMED.

GROWTH AFTER TRAUMA

JENNIFER HOBBS

burning soul
press

Calmed.

Growth After Trauma

Copyright © 2021 by Jennifer Hobbs

Cover design: MiblArt

ISBNs:

978-1-950476-28-2 (paperback)

978-1-950476-29-9 (eBook)

Published by:

Dedicated to the Cawvster. Your boots will hang forever battle!
Much love, Buff

1

FALL IN

Jen:

Who is this joker pacing the ranks, glaring at us up and down? He walks back and forth slowly, intimidatingly with his dark eyes scanning the rows of soldiers. His snide smirk sends the message that he is just looking for someone to rip into. As I stand timid and anxious, barely seventeen years old, amid a sea of unfamiliar faces, I focus on maintaining my composure and standing still. My eyes wander as I check out my surroundings. The large gymnasium is like the one at the YMCA where I used to play bitty ball. The floors are made of rubber, the lights are dim, and all I can hear is the rickety fan systems caressing us with some not-so-calming mood music. Standing in formation amongst the ranks of individuals, I am overwhelmed by the mixed odor of coffee, booze, cologne, and cigarettes.

A sergeant walks into the gym and takes position in front of the formation. "Platoon, attention!" he commands. Nervously, I scan the crowd out of my peripheral vision to confirm I'm doing the same as all the others. I wouldn't have had the slightest clue what to do, however a brief weekend of training for new recruits taught me some basic commands and movements.

"Parade, rest!" he directs us, allowing us to stand at a position more relaxed to take roll call. With my legs shoulder-width apart and my hands clasped behind my back, this is certainly not the kind of parade I've known. No one is throwing candy, no one is cheering or waving.

How does this part-time military thing work? I feel like I'm dreaming! I was just in high school yesterday. I stayed up too late last night studying for my upcoming chemistry test. Now, I'm at my first drill weekend. Everything about this seems foreign. I thought wearing the uniform that I've been so eager to wear would be more pleasant than this. This does not feel like my brother's Marine uniform I got to try on a few years ago. These ridiculous pants strap on above my belly button. Who wears their pants this high except for busy moms that rock Levi jeans?

My mind is spinning like a ballerina. Uncertainty continues after roll call as the gawking man, suited up with what appears to be an important rank, starts to walk amongst the formation of soldiers. He seems to be inspecting uniforms. I can't make out what he says to a few others. He's headed this way. Crap. I struggle to keep my eyes forward, trying to ignore his intimidating presence. The tension I'm feeling locks me up as he stops right in front of me. Uh-oh, what did I do wrong? Is my uniform okay? Did I miss a command?

He seems to be inspecting my uniform. Straining to avoid making eye contact, my stomach turns as chills work their way up my spine. The back of my neck and my ears feel hot.

"Ah, I see we have a new private today. Private Buffington," he says loudly, bringing attention to me. Others break their positions from facing forward to sneak a glance my way.

"Yes, Sergeant," I bark, irritated with the attention he has brought my way. His arm reaches out toward me, invading what I thought was my personal space. Whoa, buddy! I lose my balance as he tugs at my left side, and the sound of ripping stitches breaks the silence.

"I'm not a sergeant. You can call me Lieutenant, Private Buffington. This patch is on the wrong side. Try again." I feel my face flush with humiliation as he hands me my American flag patch. I quickly shove it in my pocket.

What? My mom just sewed that on. Apparently on the wrong side, but still. That wasn't the easiest task when you didn't know where to sew it. She had at least used the right color thread to match my uniform, but that didn't matter. That experience was memorable enough for me that I'll never forget where that patch goes.

My mom must have felt somewhat confident about sewing that patch on, as she spent eight years in the Idaho National Guard. She started as an administrative assistant before taking some online courses that enabled her to move into small engine repair. Her duties changed again later when a riot at the nearby prison broke out at the same time forest fires blazed in Idaho. So many people were mobilized for those two events, there was no one left to do the heavy wheeled mechanics at the unit, so that became her new task.

She wasn't the only one in my family who served. I come from a long line of service members—a grandfather I never met, my uncle, my biological father, and my brother. I grew up with my brother, and that was where I heard the most stories. Scott was in the Marines. Although we moved a lot during my childhood, it was not due to the military. I never lived the Army brat life. It was more due to crazy life and shitty circumstances.

There was always a part of me that was curious about the military. I felt like another person the day I tried on my brother's Marine uniform. He was reluctant to allow me to even touch it. It was a sacred uniform that was earned. I knew that from his stories of boot camp and of how he became a Marine. I was intrigued hearing about his struggles and triumphs he shared from his experiences.

My curiosity for the military grew when I learned that the military provides assistance with college tuition. There was no way my momma could pay for college. She busted her ass working two jobs to provide for Scott and me. She was a single mother for most of our lives and did not have the financial resources to fund my college.

If I wanted to go to college, I was going to have to figure out how to make that happen on my own. I'd always known that, so I had to grow up fast and learn the meaning of a hard-earned dollar. In addition to indulging myself in extracurriculars, I maintained two jobs outside of being a high school student. My hope was that in addition to my good grades, my hard work and leadership would make me more marketable for jobs.

Just before my seventeenth birthday, I made an appointment with a recruiter from the Illinois Army National Guard. A fellow classmate and friend of mine, Peter, had recently joined with the Military Occupational Specialty (MOS) code of 88M, which translates to 88 Mike, or Motor Transport Operator. As I considered what I wanted to do in the Guard, I was leaning toward the same job as Peter so I could have a familiar face in the unit. Plus, that MOS came with a $6,000 sign-on bonus! At seventeen, six grand seemed really attractive.

On February 2, 2001, my eighteenth birthday, I signed on the dotted line to serve my country as an 88M for the next eight years. I wasn't exactly sure what this journey would bring, but I was under the impression that the National Guard (*nation* being the base word here) would only be mobilized for national duties or disasters. I did not think I would see foreign soil. It had been a long time since the US was involved in a war. To me, that was just something I read about in history books. What a misconception!

As I finished the school year, life threw a few curve balls. My family was recovering from some major life changes. My mom was dealing with some circumstances that stemmed from her divorce with my stepdad, and then my grandpa passed which brought another set of issues.

My grandma and grandpa had never married. So even though he had written in the will that she could live in their house until she died or remarried, that didn't matter since his children were put in charge of the will. Against his wishes, they told her she had to move so they could sell the house. They then put all my grandma's things up for auction unless she was able to provide receipts. This included the china cabinet my grandpa had made for her. My mom had to buy back some of my grandma's most cherished possessions.

My grandmother moved in with us. We struggled during that time. Bills went unpaid, our car was repossessed, and then we received an eviction notice.

My mom had met someone online. When we were evicted, my mom struggled with the decision on what to do. She decided she wanted to relocate to Minnesota to "start over." We would have a place to live with the man she was seeing, at least until she could get on her feet again. This was devastating news to me. I didn't want to leave my school. I wanted to stay with my friends and to finish high school with them. I guilted her and begged. Against her better judgement, she allowed me to stay in Illinois and live with my twenty-one-year-old brother, Scott.

Finally, as my junior year of high school came to a close, I waited anxiously to report to basic training in Fort Leonard Wood, Missouri. When summer arrived, I packed my bags with so many unnecessary things I wouldn't touch for the next ten weeks. This was the start of many life lessons.

2

HANGRY

JEN:

HERE I AM AGAIN in this uncomfortable uniform. Man, I'm totally going to miss a whole summer break. I'm going to miss hanging out with my friends.

Reception was the first stop at basic training. Excruciatingly boring days filled with medical assessments, distribution of gear, paperwork, and learning to hurry up and wait. Loaded up in a van full of new recruits, we pulled to a stop outside a large tin-like building late one evening. We were surrounded by wooded areas with an array of eerie sounds coming from the darkness. The soldier who drove us escorted us into the tin building with ceilings that stretched two stories high. Although my vision was obscured from the shadowy darkness, I could see rows and rows of bunk beds.

A scary woman in uniform broke the silence, "Grab a bunk. Wake-up will be at 0400 hours. Be dressed and ready to go.

And whatever you do, don't be late." She tossed us each a pillow and an itchy, green wool blanket before she exited.

I timidly searched for an open spot amongst the aisles of bunks. I maneuvered around quietly because some recruits were already sleeping. I located a spot on a top bunk, grabbed my toothbrush, and headed to find the latrine, or what I'd always known as a bathroom. I quickly identified its location since it was a revolving door with light streaming out of it as other recruits came in and out. I entered and quickly realized I was going to have to wait my turn behind this line of females. With about eight females trying to share three sinks, the silence that continued was so peculiar. Eight females in one bathroom typically wasn't a quiet setting. I wondered if everyone else was as nervous as I was.

I was no punk, or at least I didn't think so. But after all the stories my brother told me about his Marine basic training, I prepared myself for the worst.

I needed to get some sleep. Dear God, that blanket was brutal! I kicked it off, trying to escape the torture. Staring up at the ceiling, I struggled to calm my thoughts. Not only was I anticipating what tomorrow would be like, but I was thinking about my family also. That spring was rough for us, and I didn't know what to expect when I returned to normal life. Would my mom be back? Would I still be living with Scott for my senior year of high school?

The 4:00 a.m. wake-up call was loud and clear as the lights came on and the angry voices bellowing through the building demanded, "Get up out of bed! You have exactly ten minutes to be in formation!"

I didn't have time to dress and wait in line for a sink. *Alright then, skip the toothbrush and just put your boots on, Jen.* I scrambled to put on my uniform and get my hair into a bun. *Crap, I should have practiced this.* I managed to get it to hold and reached back to feel hair sticking out where it shouldn't be. *This is definitely not up to military standards. Screw it, I gotta go.* I hustled to the door and entered the darkness of the early morning.

Dang, that's a lot of people! Confused recruits came from all directions. We all looked like we were trying to figure out where to fall in to formation. Once we were standing in formation, I smelled the crisp morning air flowing from trees around us. It sounds so calm, yet no part of me felt calm.

After waiting for what seemed like forever, a sergeant called us to attention and marched us into a long hallway. It was stuffy and packed with the tired new recruits. A few seemed like they'd done it before; most seemed scared shitless. Struggling to stand, I locked my legs to make sure I was stiff as a board. I was hangry, and my stomach was fiercely growling. My body started to tingle, and feelings of light-headedness crept in slowly.

I recognized the feeling.

Oh crap! Don't do this, Jennifer. Not now, not here. There is nowhere to sit down. Get yourself together!

Panic rushed through my veins. I started to see black spots and felt myself drifting away.

CRAP!

"I am going to pass out," I whispered to the girl in front of me.

"Shh," she responded impatiently and didn't turn around.

Falling forward, I was numb and couldn't stop myself. *Awesome! I fainted on the first day of reception. Impressive! Impressively embarrassing!*

"Get up, Private, this is no time to take a nap!" a tall, angry, and impatient sergeant demanded of me. I slowly tried to lift my head out of the horizontal position. *What is happening?*

Another sergeant, smaller in stature and clearly older,

briskly walked over and knelt at my side. He told me not to get up. Sergeant Angry walked away without saying another word, yet his look of disgust said it all. I lay back down. *Oh, praise Jesus! Thank you, stranger!* I was about to fall right back out again.

"Private, you okay?" he asked with concern, yet still held a certain tone to keep up his image and intimidation.

I struggled to respond. "Yes, Sergeant, just got dizzy." I managed to stand up and return to my place in line. Finally, the line started to move after they opened the dining facility doors, commonly referred to as the DFAC. I was close enough to the doors that I could smell the delicious food and seriously felt like I hadn't eaten in days. My body felt light, my stomach was sick, and I was a bit confused about what had just happened. I continued to pep talk myself to make it through the line. *Almost there, Jennifer, you'll be okay! Get it together. You will eat and be fine.*

As soon as I hit the threshold of the DFAC doors, the gust of air from the open windows hit my soul like magic. *Finally! Oxygen! Yes!* The air blew through the DFAC with the same pleasure of a cool summer morning, but then my surroundings didn't match the pleasurable breeze and the aroma of the food I was about to max out on.

Focusing on not locking my legs, I waited at parade rest for the line to move closer to the chow line entrance. Failing to maintain my focus looking straight ahead, my eyes wandered to the trays of food other recruits were indulging in. Not sure *indulging* is a great way to describe it since enjoying a meal was challenging when sergeants were walking around hollering orders.

"Hurry up, Private! You don't have time to butter your toast. What do you think this is, Sunday morning brunch? Let's go." The voice sounded familiar. I looked over and realized it was. That was Sergeant Angry. *Oh shit. He just saw me. Look forward. Act cool.*

I made it through the line without making another scene or getting attacked by Sergeant Angry. After I got some food in my stomach, things turned around, and I was feeling way different. I was a bit distraught about what had transpired in the last hour, but I had to get over it.

I soon fell into the role that soldiers are expected to follow: I listened. I obeyed. In basic training, I had a small glimpse of what was expected of me in active duty. We trained and prepared for what was to come.

Rumors at reception spread fast about the shark attack coming for us. *Shark attack* was the term used to describe the moment when the drill sergeants would arrive to pick us up. From there we would head to our training unit where we would complete ten weeks of basic training.

The day arrived. Loaded up with two duffel bags of gear, half of which I couldn't tell you what it was, I heard a vehicle getting closer. I wasn't sure what it was, but it didn't sound like the bus we were expecting.

Two large semis pulling cattle trailers came around the corner and turned toward our direction. *What is happening? These are definitely not buses. My best friend's dad is a farmer. I know what these are. Why are they here? Are they hauling cattle around on this base?*

When we saw uniforms through the holes of the cattle trailer, it quickly became evident that they were here for us. I was shocked and confused. Intense intimidation rose as the drill sergeants stepped off the cattle trailers. Some came off slowly with an uncanny demeanor, creeping around with a gaze of complete disgust.

Other drill sergeants jumped off the cattle trailer like vicious pit bulls. They all came out attacking immediately with demands and directions for us to follow. I was freaking out and looking around frantically, trying to keep up with the list of things they expected out of us. Drill sergeants screamed at us to grab our gear and hustle. I carried one duffel bag on my back and another in my hands, trying to get my ass on that trailer as fast as I could. The weight of the gear was shocking, but adrenaline helped, and I managed through. In the midst of it all, I heard crying, more than one cry. Some people couldn't keep it in and released what most of us were feeling. The drill sergeants simultaneously talked mad trash the whole ride. I could barely keep up with all they were saying.

"Hold your bag and put your face in it! Beat your face! Don't look at me! Are you looking at me? Are we friends? Do we hang out?" I heard one yell.

"No, Drill Sergeant," I heard a female reply.

Her response seemed almost joyful, not completely freaked out like I was.

"Are you smiling at me right now? Is that funny? Wait a minute. What's your name? Ah, I see. Loocher here thinks it's funny. I've got something for you, Loocher!" I heard a drill sergeant say.

In an amused tone, she replied, "It's Louche, Drill Sergeant."

Laughing, the drill sergeant said, "Yeah, okay Loocher. Stop playing! You are not from France! Get your face back in your bag!" How was she not freaked out?

The trailers came to a stop, and my arms hurt from holding up all the weight. "Get off my trailer now! You have ten seconds to get out of my face. Ten ... nine ... eight ..." He continued as we fumbled over one another and tried to find the exit without dropping all our gear.

We ran off the cattle trailers, and there were more drill sergeants! *Jesus! How many are there?* They hollered out numbers indicating which platoon we were going to be in, while others screamed commands. In a unit of about ninety soldiers, we were divided into platoons of around thirty people.

"You will be assigned a battle buddy. You will go absolutely everywhere with your battle buddy. By no means, will you go anywhere without them. If your battle buddy gets smoked, you get smoked. Keep each other squared away!" Drill Sergeant Jeanz demanded. "Buffington, you will be with Loocher."

Are you kidding me? I have to be battle buddies with the chick who thinks everything is hilarious? It was the same chick from the cattle trailer who had the audacity to correct the crazy pit bulls when they mispronounced her name. She was around the same age as me and had brown hair. She could tie up her bun better than I could do mine. She was from Oregon and seemed to find everything rather humorous.

SHE WAS A GREAT BATTLE BUDDY. We were smoked so much, we lived in the push-up position. It was rough, but after a while, we almost enjoyed it. She helped me to lighten up and appreciate the challenges. We both enjoyed the sense of humor of our platoon drill sergeants, Drill Sergeant Jeanz and Drill Sergeant Sanchez. They were good leaders. And although they scared the shit out of me most of the summer, I knew they were in it to be influential and to train good soldiers.

I met a few other great battles that summer, girls from all over the nation with different stories and backgrounds. One girl in my room was also from Illinois, and we daydreamed about plans to hang out when we got out of there.

It was surreal to be on summer break before my senior year in a completely different environment than any of my friends. While they were swimming, tanning, fishing, and living the dream, I was learning so much about myself. I learned I was stronger than I thought I was, both physically and emotionally. I mean, don't get me wrong—at first, I learned how out of shape I was. I think many of us did, and the drill sergeants loved watching the horror.

From somersaulting downhill, bear crawling uphill, and getting smoked in knee-high grass called the Tick Farm, it all worked well together to break you down, only to build you back up. At least, that's what I think the purpose is. Your mind is stronger than your body, but it is important that you figure that out.

It was raining, and the drill sergeants ordered us to go inside and put on our wet weather gear. Our wet weather gear consisted of a jacket and pants to put on over our uniforms. As we stood in the rain, shivering from the temperature drop, the misery became a tad bit more bearable when I heard, "Well, well, well, look who we have here." Laughing, Drill Sergeant Jeanz said, "Check it out, Drill Sergeant Sanchez. Batman came to join us in formation." Glancing over to see what he was talking about, I realized a recruit came out with his military-issued poncho on rather than his wet weather gear.

Chiming in with complete pleasure, Drill Sergeant Sanchez replied, "Well, my God! Finally! Force protection has arrived!" Just as he said that, with the absolute best of timing, another recruit ran out of the barracks, also wearing a poncho.

Despite being miserable from the cold, I was starting to enjoy this. "Well, would you look at that, Drill Sergeant Sanchez. It seems he called for his sidekick, Robin. I tell you what, Batman, I want you to run around this entire formation shouting, 'I'm Batman! Come, Robin, to the Batcave!' while we march to chow."

The drill sergeants lost it, and some of us recruits couldn't help but let out a chuckle. The drill sergeants didn't like that we were laughing along with them. They became ticked off and didn't skip a beat with their intimidation. Their fearlessness was something they seemed to always carry with them. They were squared away, swift, and thorough.

Day in and day out, I woke up and rushed to compose myself prior to heading to formation. Some days were okay, most days just plain sucked. One morning, as all of us females were woken up in a hurry, we heard a commotion coming from the hall. Apparently, the fireguard didn't wake us up on time, and the entire bay of females was late to formation. The meanest drill sergeant was on Sunday morning duty solo. I swear he had it out for females. I bet he intentionally had the fireguard *not* wake us, he was that bitter.

As we all dashed out of the barracks, I saw all the males were in formation already. Some glanced our way with condescending looks, others were too tired to care. Drill Sergeant Benton stood there, hands on his hips, cursing under his breath as we scrambled to our places.

It was Sunday, so it was the only day we had some sort of relaxation. We didn't relax though. We cleaned, we did groundskeeping, and if we signed up for a religious service, we were bused there for it. Drill Sergeant Benton took roll call, then dismissed the males to the barracks.

He paraded back and forth telling us how pitiful we were and how others would suffer from our lack of attention to details. He then marched us females to the Tick Farm. The Tick Farm was a waist-high field full of spiky foliage and ticks that were dying to suck your blood. He smoked us for about thirty minutes, enjoying every minute of it. Up and down, side to side, rolls, somersaults, push-ups, you name it. It was one of the worst smokings I got at basic, probably because he was so outraged by us.

DURING THOSE TEN WEEKS, some recruits couldn't cut it. Some left crying, others left faking suicidal thoughts, resulting in losing their shoelaces, and some had legitimate reasons. Some sissies thought those techniques to bow out would be successful. However, they didn't realize that when you were injured or "held over" for any reason, you didn't catch a quick ride home. Instead, you dealt with the brutality of hurry up and wait while your case was pending. They definitely didn't try to hurry for you. *Way to bow out of your commitment.* That's how they weeded out the weak, which was good. You didn't need someone who didn't want to be there sitting in a foxhole next to you.

I was not a stellar recruit in physical fitness. I could've been better, but I struggled with mind over matter. I barfed at every organized physical training assessment. The anxiety got the best of me. Yes, I could be a sissy at times, I guess. Other times, I killed it.

Toward the end of basic training, we went through weapons qualification with an M16 semiautomatic rifle. We trained for shooting distances twenty-five to three hundred meters using pop-up targets. That was awesome! I had never shot a real gun before, unlike some of the cocky recruits. They were overly confident in their skills, whereas I was completely in the dark. I mean, I could look cool in a picture, and spout off *Scarface* quotes, but I certainly didn't know what I was doing. So, I listened closely and learned how to be the best shot I could be.

The final day on the range as we were qualifying, I was ticked off that one of my targets didn't pop up. I knew it didn't because my drill sergeant and I counted to ourselves while I shot from both the prone and the foxhole positions. When I finished, I was excited about how well I did, but my first complaint didn't even have the chance to escape my mouth before Drill Sergeant Sanchez said, "That was only forty-nine targets. I counted it. You didn't get fifty pop-ups."

"I know, Drill Sergeant. I counted them too," I agreed.

"You did good, Private Buffington. Now keep your rifle down range and head that way," he said as he pointed toward the same entry point I came in.

I was ticked off that I was cheated out of one target, but I felt proud of myself. I did better that day than I did any of our days on the range. Hard work paid off. Listening and being open-minded as a learner paid off. As I carried my rifle to the clearing barrel, I heard the range tower intercom turn on and say, "Lane seven shot expert, forty-seven out of fifty."

That was me! I was on lane seven. I heard them make that announcement only one other time that day. *Look at me. Scott and my mom would be so proud of me*, I thought.

I cleared my rifle to make sure no rounds were left in the chamber and started to walk off the range. I was sweating bullets that were rolling into my eyes and stinging. As I removed my Kevlar, I heard more than one voice say, "Oh my God, it's a girl."

I shocked some that day as I walked off the range and removed my Kevlar. Whispers and stares continued as I made my way to my canteen to hydrate. *Simmer down dudes. Maybe next time you won't let a set of tits fool you.*

The day of the gas chamber was the absolute worst. Platoons were split into groups of ten people to enter the chamber at one time. I was at the end of my line of ten. I had heard that was the worst place to be since you would be in there the longest amount of time. They made you take in the gas for a while, snot pouring out of your nose, dripping down to your knees before it hit the ground. My eyes burned so bad, I thought I would lose my eyesight.

When they finally gave the command to "don your mask," the torture had consumed me. Fumbling around without the ability to see, I secured my mask and got it on. Suddenly, I could see the light shining through. I heard the commotion of soldiers as they rushed out, pushing their way to the daylight from the exit door.

Finally outside, I took off my mask. Trying to regain my composure, I was hacking up my lungs like I was dying. Tears poured from my eyes, and it didn't make them feel any better to rub them. As things got a bit more clear around me, I saw soldiers all around me with snot pouring from their noses as they gasped for air. Some rookies were being a tad bit dramatic. Either they were exaggerating, or they had been babied their whole lives and didn't know what struggle was.

You didn't become a soldier until you earned it. You had to navigate warrior challenges during field training exercise and go on a long ruck march to the destination where you ran through simulated combat missions. On the last evening, you ventured out into the darkness, performing different tactical operations on foot. Then you went through a simulated attack with small arms fire and loud explosions as you low-crawled under barbed wire.

At the end, you knelt during the rite of passage ceremony. It was then that I received my Army Values card. I put that tag on my dog tags with pride. The Army Values are a part of my life. Loyalty, duty, respect, selfless service, honor, integrity, and personal courage. *I did it! I am an American soldier.*

My grandmother and mother came to see me graduate basic training into soldierhood. I returned to my hometown a different person, a better person. I had learned self-discipline, hard work, integrity, and so much more. My mother visited for a short time before returning to Minnesota, where she had moved prior to me attending basic.

I started my senior year of high school and filled my time with work and extracurricular activities. I served as student body president and was a member of the Pom-Pom Squad, Pep Club, Spanish Club, and other groups. I always thought my chances at college would be guaranteed if I showed that I was involved and was a hard worker with great potential.

Living with my brother didn't exactly work out for us. After an argument one day, I decided to move. A friend of mine and her family had a spare room since her two older sisters had moved out. They were gracious enough to allow me to move into one of the bedrooms. They treated me with kindness and supported me during that time in my life.

One day at school, I was unexpectedly called into the principal's office. She proceeded to point out how I was a "bad influence" since I left early from school and that I should be a better example for others. I was a bit taken aback. *Excuse me? So, you are referring to the fact that I leave two hours early?* I then pointed out to her that I had a community service class that required me to report to a local Alzheimer's Unit that I served at. The last class of the day was my study hall, so I was allowed to not come back. She reiterated how I was not being a good example leaving. She then compared me to one of my peers.

I reminded her that my peer she referred to had a used Camaro that his parents had paid for, whereas I was driving a Mercury Tracer that I had gotten a cosigned loan to purchase. She didn't have much to say after I pointed that out to her. I was dismissed, feeling as though she was judging me, and left the room to resume my senior year.

As the Student Body President, the senior class president

and I did the daily announcements on the intercom. One day halfway through my senior year, we had just finished the morning announcements, and I exited the small room in the main office and headed to class.

"Hey Jennifer, the mother of a friend of yours mentioned that this might be something you would be interested in," she said as she handed me a paper that read "James E. Heinzel Scholarship" in bold black letters at the top.

I was completely caught off guard. We typically exchanged common greetings when I passed by because I usually had to hustle on to class. Surprised, I smiled and said thank you. As I walked out the office, I skimmed through the application. Right away, I noticed the words, "students under the poverty level may qualify to apply." Those words instantly caught my attention.

Ugh ... those words ... those lame circumstances that I'd always been labeled under. That was one aspect of my life that gave me even more of a reason to persevere. I was tired of being labeled and judged based on my childhood, the choices of those I loved, and the struggles we'd grown through. Whether people wanted to acknowledge it or not, this label put preconceived notions in a lot of people's perceptions.

With the help of my friend's beloved mother, whom I'd known and loved since I was in the fourth grade, I prepared what I needed for my application. She kept me motivated and gave me hope on what the opportunity could do for me, reminding me of what I've worked so hard for. I am forever grateful.

Even though my mother was six hours away, she continued to call and worry. She continued to love hard and still struggled herself. Things were strange since I hadn't done life without my mother until she moved. She taught Scott and me well though. Her choices throughout that time may not have been the best thing for her or for us, but we survived.

A few months later, I was about to flee to class after finishing up the announcements when the superintendent called me into his office. *Um, what? Did he just say my name? Am I hearing things?* There were over six hundred students in that school. He motioned for me to come into his office, and I cautiously proceeded with a smile on my face.

With complete seriousness on his face and in his demeanor, he began, "Well Jennifer, we here at this district pride ourselves in our ability to train great kids that will turn around and contribute to society, and hopefully, our community. The James E. Heinzel Scholarship is a great opportunity for some that don't have as many financial options for their hopes and dreams to attend college. This year we had a lot of applicants. It was certainly not easy. I would like you to know that the board of the committee chose you to be the recipient of this year's scholarship. We are proud of you, and we look forward to seeing who you become."

I was flabbergasted. Hot tears filled my eyes. The superintendent looked at me through his glasses that sat low on his nose above his warmhearted smile. I tried to contain the tears of joy pouring down my face. I felt the warmth from my tears rolling down, and I knew my mascara was running. I couldn't hold back. He seemed to understand how much this meant to me as he smiled, offered me a Kleenex, and allowed me a moment to take it in.

All my life I had been a struggling student. I faced challenges that stemmed from growing up in financial distress as well as childhood events that left scars. I had trained myself to focus on the good and tried not to get hung up on the past. My mom had taught me that as long as you have love, you have everything.

While my friends sat at the lunch table and talked about being oh-so-tired from staying up late binge-watching television, I was that girl who chimed in with an awkward comment they couldn't relate to. "I am so tired too! My mom's car is going to be repo'd. Last night, she parked in the garage, and the repo man came by. We had the lights all turned off, ducking down low so he couldn't see us. He tried hard too! He had his flashlight out looking in windows and everything." I stopped when I realized their body language was sending me the vibe that I should shut my mouth because no one knew what I was talking about.

"Oh my gosh, that happened to us last week," my friend Holly laughed as she said it out loud. Completely relating to the chaotic feeling it gives you, I laughed with her.

Things looked a lot different from that perspective. My upbringing taught me a lot and made me a better person. Things were never easy and far from handed to me. I had to work for everything and trained myself to be resilient.

In the end, it all paid off. The scholarship I received was meant to fund my tuition for four years. However, since I had already secured four years of tuition by joining the Army National Guard, the scholarship paid for my room and board for four years while I attended college. *Somebody pinch me! Is this really happening?*

3

TWO WEEKS' NOTICE

Hobbs:

WHAT ELSE DO you do when you're bored? Join the Army, of course. That's what my buddy Shaun and I did. During our crotch rocket days, we spent a lot of time riding around, living what we thought was our best life. Sounds normal for eighteen-year-old boys, right? One day, he mentioned that he was thinking of joining the military.

"Hey, me too," I said because I had totally been considering it. There you have it, decision made. We signed up the next day and headed out within a few days to start processing in St. Louis, Missouri, at a place called the Military Entrance Processing Station, or MEPS. It was in a large building in downtown St. Louis, and the entire floor was filled with military branch offices. The signs on the doors indicated which branch. Other doors read medical exams, and there was a room where you stood before our nation's flag and were sworn into the military.

After waddling like a duck during a medical exam, taking a piss test, and eating some awesome food in the dining area, we swore in as soldiers of the Illinois Army National Guard. We were set to go to basic training and advanced individual training (AIT) together, but our plan did not work out the way we expected. Just before we were to ship out, Shaun broke his foot and was put on med hold. Med hold is the shitty in-between you get stuck in as you transition from some medical status before returning to training. The experience is different for all, but not commonly known as a positive experience. No one wants to be there, well, of course, unless you are a soldier wanting to go back home.

I went to basic training solo in the dead of winter. My first day of basic training was New Year's Eve of 1998. Ain't that a bitch! Happy freaking New Year! I was stuck there, freezing in the Army without my buddy Shaun.

I wasn't happy to continue basic training without him, but I did what I had to do. I listened to them attempt to bark out orders for me to follow. I didn't take well to orders. I never have. I floated through basic and shrugged it off like summer basket-ball camp.

Then on graduation day, my dad, my brother, and Shaun came to Fort Leonard Wood, and I was released to go with them after graduation for a quick leave. We stayed in a hotel and didn't do a whole lot. I enjoyed a steak dinner and then we just chilled back in our room. The leave was short lived, but it was nice to get a break.

When it was time for my dad and brother to head out, I said goodbye, and Shaun drove me back to the base so I could return for AIT. As we pulled up, I was confused why people weren't gathering into formation or at least waiting around for it.

There were a few soldiers walking around, still with their

families, laughing, smiling, and enjoying themselves. Who enjoys themselves right at that moment of return? I wasn't laughing and certainly not smiling, as I had to put these damn Army boots on this morning and pack up my civilian clothes.

As Shaun was about to leave, I asked him to stick around for a minute while I checked out what was going on. Just then, I recognized another soldier, Diego, from my platoon. I walked over to him with a confused look plastered on my face.

"What's going on?" I questioned.

"They are giving us a few more days of leave if you can have your parents sign you out," Diego broke the news to me.

"What? Are you shitting me?! My dad just left the state! He's probably already made it to the border," I exhaled with frustration.

I was pissed to say the least. Diego clearly couldn't relate since he was over eighteen and could check himself out. Changing quickly from confused, to surprised, to pissed off, I started pacing back and forth trying to process this. Then, I caught a glimpse of Martinez, another battle buddy, who was still with his family. I got a genius idea. I approached him and chatted him up while we were alone.

I mentioned my plan to Martinez, and an apprehensive smirk spread across his face. His eyes nervously darted back and forth between his dad and me. His dad didn't speak a lick of English. Although Martinez was hesitant about the risky plan, he was down with it, and we proceeded to the barracks to sign me out for leave, with my borrowed dad.

We walked to the barracks and approached the soldier on fireguard. I put on my loving-son performance. I put my arm around my short Mexican pops. "Dad, we are going to have so much fun." He just nodded and smiled. The soldier on fireguard stared straight in my eyes, clearly questioning my claim, but there wasn't much he could say, and he knew it.

The plan worked! I thanked Martinez, shook his pops's hand, and I was on my way with Shaun again, but this time to St. Louis, Missouri. On a whim, Diego decided to join us for our unplanned adventure.

My older brother attended college in St. Louis, so we stayed there and hit up the downtown nightlife. With our obvious military buzz cuts, our fake IDs worked easily. It had been a long time since I had seen so many people, so many lights, and so much action. I was so pumped to be out and tried to enjoy every minute of it. We smashed those bars downtown!

After a blowout on Shaun's car, we caught a Greyhound so we could get back to AIT before we were late. The bus was delayed which threatened our ability to report back on time. So, we scored a taxi all the way from St. Louis to Fort Leonard Wood. Diego sat next to me, shaving in the taxi on the way. That wasn't something I had to worry about at that point in my life. I could usually wait a few days to shave, well at least I thought so. But let's face it, I wasn't exactly exceeding the Army standards.

I completed AIT and started the part-time citizen/soldier gig with the National Guard while I maintained my full-time manager position at McDonald's. I attended drill one weekend a month. Our platoon usually drilled at a separate location than the rest of the unit. The other platoons reported for drill at the main headquarters in Paris, Illinois. We were the detachment, and there were only a handful of people that drilled there.

For a few years, I continued this citizen/soldier gig, and I did somewhat enjoy it. It could be pretty boring at times. Other times it was exciting, like on our brief two-week rotation in Belize. We didn't have much purpose in Belize. We were just the National Guard, setting things up for those to come. I was there only a few weeks. We didn't have much to do, and our time was spent with ridiculous purpose. I remember we secured a flatbed of beer. We also gathered bamboo to create what would be the tiki bar for soldiers to come. We had very little to do. Then we left and returned back home.

Drill stateside was usually just doing preventative maintenance checks and services (PMCS) on the trucks. We got the job done during the day and got buck wild after hours.

At the end of one of the drills, I was minding my own business. Ha-ha ... not really. I was being an idiot. Our platoon leader, Lieutenant Donnell got tired of my arrogant mouthiness and started smoking me. He had me doing all these push-ups, and at first, I put up with it. I was in the best shape of my life, so ... whatever, I let him have his power trip. I could play this game too. In classy form, I mouthed off the whole time.

I could feel the previous night's late-night drinks creeping into my throat, as I held back from vomiting all over. Others were watching, waiting to see what was going to happen. Some were just standing there trying not to laugh, including my platoon sergeant.

"Screw this, I quit. I'm giving my two weeks," I said as I climbed to my feet from the push-up position. That was it. I was done. I wasn't putting up with that crap.

After some time had passed, I considered returning to drill. Just as I was thinking about going back to attend a drill, a certified letter showed up in the mail with an honorable discharge from the Army National Guard. *Hell yeah. That works for me!*

Then one day, I was working, and a friend of mine came in to get something to eat and asked me, "Hey, did you hear your old unit is getting deployed?"

"No. Are you serious?" I questioned in shock. *What the fuck? My unit I was in with Shaun is getting deployed?*

He replied, "Yeah, they are leaving in like four weeks or something."

"No kidding," I responded calmly, but I was feeling

completely beside myself. *What is happening? They can't go without me.*

I hadn't even finished my shift at work before I messaged one of my battle buddies to get the first sergeant's phone number. My old platoon sergeant was now the first sergeant. I called him to let him know that I wanted to join the unit on deployment.

He responded with, "Ya know, Donnell is now our Captain, right?" He was referring to the same joker who had smoked me when he was a lieutenant and I had quit.

I confirmed, "Yeah, I'll be alright." Alright? Maybe not the best response, but it was the best I could do. What I meant was, it was fine, water under the bridge. I had grown a bit and acknowledged that I could be persistent when I wanted to be. I could also be quite a shithead at times.

He told me he would make some calls and see what he could do. He called me back later that night. I had to write a letter to a high-ranking official in the Illinois National Guard. I stayed up late to finish that letter. A few days later, I headed back to MEPS, the processing center in St. Louis, Missouri, for a second time.

I had only three or four weeks to get shit in order before the unit deployed. When I returned from MEPS, I told my mom that I was being deployed with the 1544th Transportation Company to Iraq. She didn't question it, and I wasn't exactly being honest. I knew what I had to do, or at least what I wanted to do. I was pretty good at doing what I wanted to. I notified my job of my upcoming deployment. Then it was time to report back to Paris, Illinois.

4

A VALENTINE'S DAY TO REMEMBER

JEN:

THE SUMMER after my senior year, I headed back to Fort Leonard Wood, Missouri, for AIT to learn my job as an 88M. Ugh, I did not miss those bugs or the Missouri heat!

I spent my days training on how to drive a Light Medium Tactical Vehicle (LMTV). AIT was far different than my basic training. They were tough, but not half as hard core as my basic training leaders. We spent our days training on various convoy and formation techniques. One week was dedicated to qualifying on the tractor trailers. I was not as skilled in those.

While I was at AIT, my mother and stepdad reignited their love for one another. This time, however, they started by building their friendship, valuing one another as friends before moving into a relationship. It had been three years since their divorce, and they both had learned so much and couldn't find happiness without one another. When my mom lived in Minnesota, Scott and I continued a relationship with Mike even though we struggled with the pain from their divorce. So, I was thrilled that they were back together.

Unfortunately, it wasn't long before I had to head out again, and I missed out on their reunification. It was time for me to pack my bags and prepare for my first year of college. My first-pick college did not accept my application, and I didn't have my heart set on any others. I decided to go to the same college as my friend whose mother helped me obtain the application for the scholarship I was awarded.

My mother, grandmother, and I loaded up and headed to Dekalb, Illinois, to drop me off at Northern Illinois University (NIU). The soldier in my mom came out that day. My dorm room was on the tenth floor, and the line for the elevator was ridiculous.

"Alright, let's take the stairs," she said matter-of-factly.

"What? For ten flights? Mom, seriously?" I laughed as I questioned her.

She looked at me like I was confused and headed toward the stairwell. After multiple trips up and down those ten flights of stairs, hauling the weight of my belongings, we finished, and I was beside myself as my mom was still in beast mode. She's so badass, and it's times like those that remind me!

I kissed my grandma and momma goodbye. I turned around and looked up at the huge dorm building in front of me. As I gazed up at the twelve stories of my new home, the stimulation of sounds around me disappeared. For just a moment, I was disconnected from the hustling and bustling around me. As I snapped out of my trance, I smiled at my mother with excitement. She smiled back. Time to unpack. Hello freedom!

I managed to maintain good grades while I indulged in college freedom with new friends. I completed my first semester as a freshman and started the second semester.

February 14, 2003, Valentine's Day, I received an unexpected phone call.

Walking back from the community dorm room showers, mentally preparing myself for a big test I had in a few hours, I heard our landline phone ringing. *Well, that's strange.* We didn't typically get calls on our landline.

Apprehensive, I answered the phone with a puzzled tone. "Hello?"

"Buff, is that you?" the unfamiliar voice asked. In the Army, I'm Buff, short for my maiden name, Buffington. After confirming that it was me, I quickly concluded that it was one of my sergeants from my unit. He explained that our unit was being mobilized and directed me to withdraw from school and get things in order.

Filled with so many emotions of the unknown, I couldn't stop thinking about it on my long walk to class. I entered the auditorium filled with over a hundred students. I was typically the go-getter who headed toward the front of the room to get a close seat. I didn't like to sit in the back row, especially when I was far away in an auditorium. That day was different for me since it started so strangely with that phone call. It wouldn't leave my mind, and I kept imagining various scenarios of what was to come. I couldn't even bring myself to follow my normal routine, and I took a seat toward the back. I needed to calm these thoughts and feel more at ease. I had to focus on this test.

Palms sweating, heart racing, I tried to read the questions. I couldn't focus. I reread the questions multiple times before I could decide on an answer or even comprehend what it was asking. Struggling to separate the test from my current personal dilemma, unrelenting thoughts consumed me. I heard papers flipping as students around me turned the pages, and I panicked a bit. I flinched at each sneeze or cough. Then a flicker from a bulb that needed replaced caught my attention. I was unable to concentrate.

Finally, I finished the test and headed to the front to give it to the instructor. I waited in the line with other students, wondering what I would say to him about my not returning to class. He was an older, energetic fella.

I approached him and handed my test to him. "This morning I got a call that my Army National Guard unit is getting mobilized. I have to report next week, so I'm not sure I'll be back. I'll make sure to email you to let you know." I could only imagine what my face looked like as I tried to get that out. A frightened nineteen-year-old citizen/soldier, standing there with turmoil in my eyes and body language.

Suddenly, he shot up out of his chair, pulled himself to attention, body straight, arms to his sides, and heels together. He looked me straight in the eyes with what felt like empathy and respect. He slowly raised his right arm and saluted me with his chin held high.

"Godspeed soldier." He bid me farewell. I smiled and walked away slowly feeling far more confused since the call. Time to start the process of withdrawing from school. I had to pack all my stuff and break the lame news to my friends. I had to tell my teachers and the scholarship board.

The walk back from class was such a blur. As I passed by all my incredible surroundings that had been the home of my first college experience, I couldn't even reminisce and enjoy the walk home. I was completely consumed with what was ahead of me.

The goodbyes with my friends were difficult. They recorded a farewell video for me on my camcorder that broke my heart to watch. Tears stung my eyes as I watched my home-girls get farther away in my rearview mirror, waving goodbye as they tried to smile through their anguish. This was the last time

I drove away from college at NIU. I felt emotions I had never felt in the nineteen years of my life.

My unit was mobilized for five days. We packed up everything and prepared our trucks for transportation. We had our medical exams and completed all the paperwork needed for us to deploy, such as life insurance information. After five days, we were dismissed and told that we were not deploying at this time. They explained that our unit would be on high alert but that we could go home. What the hell did that mean? I withdrew from school. Where was I supposed to go?

My college didn't let me back in since I had withdrawn, and I was left living at home again. I became resentful that a bunch of other soldiers were able to return to college after we were released. I didn't know what I should have done differently, but the shoulda-coulda-wouldas weren't going to get me anywhere. So, time to move on.

I lived at home again for a few months and quickly enrolled in a community college about an hour away from home for the upcoming summer semester.

I found it hard to "fit in" to a typical population as a citizen/soldier. It's so weird to refer to it as a "citizen/soldier" because at the time, I didn't see the disconnection.

It is an emotional struggle, as well as an external struggle. There will always be people that will doubt you. As a female soldier, I was definitely disregarded at times.

There was a time that I requested time off from my employer in advance. The employer acted surprised when I pointed out that I was scheduled during the weekend I asked off.

He looked at me with confusion when I told him, "I can't work that weekend. I asked for that off because I have drill weekend."

"Drill what?" he questioned.

"I told you, I am in the Army National Guard. I need that weekend off for our drill duty."

"Oh yeah, someone's got to do the paperwork," he replied with sarcasm.

Oh, my goodness. These are the ignorant comments that people, even non-soldiers, have to deal with from their employers. Then you are expected to drive on and continue with what your job or mission is. Talk about a misunderstanding.

I SUCCESSFULLY ENROLLED into college classes to where I was able to attend some for both the summer semester of 2003 and the fall semester of 2003 before I received that same dreaded phone call again on November 11, 2003, Veterans Day. Our unit was getting mobilized for deployment. This time it was definitely go time.

November 11th. At that time in my military career, the significance of Veterans Day didn't mean a whole lot to me, as it doesn't for most nineteen-year-olds. We were given three weeks to prepare for what was expected to be a year-long deployment starting on December 7th, the anniversary of Pearl Harbor. Man, the Army really knows how to choose days with significance to shake our world.

On December 7th, I was driving alone, in uniform, hustling to report to the armory. As I rushed into Paris, late, I was struck with a complication a few miles out. Crap—cherries and berries in my rearview mirror. The red and blue lights slowed me down immediately.

Of course, I was getting pulled over, and I was going to be late for formation. What a way to start the deployment! After a quick stop, he quickly realized that I was reporting to the local Transportation National Guard Armory for the beginning of what would end up being our fifteen-month deployment.

"Good Luck. God Bless," he said with a kind goodbye as he handed me my warning ticket.

December 2003 was one of those pivotal periods in life that changed everything for me. I felt like I had been snatched out of my life and deported to another incomprehensible planet. I was surrounded by one hundred sixty individuals I didn't know. They were mostly from small towns in central Illinois, so we had that in common. Other than that, we were starting a whole new life experience together—one that most people would never endure or understand.

Things looked much different than basic training or AIT. People were not strung out—yet—or barking orders constantly. I looked around and could see some people consumed on their cell phones already, but others were talking and laughing together.

I caught a glimpse of this crazy ginger, Ryan Hobbs, I recognized from one of my first drills. *Holy shit! Is it seriously him? The crazy, red-headed, headbanger bus driver? Good God, it is!* I had only seen him at one drill before I went to basic training. Spirited fellow with a smile that perpetually glazed his face from ear to ear. This was not an exaggeration. The man radiated laughter and humor; it was attractive and addicting. Well, it definitely was for me.

I remembered him from a few years ago. I was warily sitting on the bus early one drill weekend in my fresh new BDUs (battle dress uniform), when on steps this crazy dude fired up at 7:30 a.m. "I'm driving the bus today, enjoy the complimentary music." The ginger pops an audio cassette tape into the old bus deck. I was certainly not expecting some headbanger crap at 7:30 in the morning!

Are you kidding me right now? Dear God, what did I get myself into joining the military? At that point I was really doubting my life decisions as I sat in the window seat and hoped I would make it safely to wherever we were going. I was still so new. I had no idea what to expect, but it certainly wasn't an early morning ride with death metal.

I never got to meet Hobbs that weekend. I went to basic training, and he never returned—until now. I was about to make sure he knew who I was this time.

I crushed real hard on Hobbs. He was rambunctious, and he seemed to dig the game I was throwing down. I may have been a bit aggressive with my late-night visits to his bunk and all my amazingness—nothing dirty, just me, as real as it gets. I had jokes for days and stories. OH, THE STORIES! He got used to them as they usually started with, "And this one time, me and my friend Megan ..."

He seemed to enjoy me, but maybe not as much as I was captivated by him. I wanted to get to know him a tad bit more. Okay, *tad bit* is a lie. I wanted to sweep him off his feet and make him fall in love with me. Although Hobbs seemed like he was ready to jump with me, we had a few challenges ahead of this potential relationship—we were both dating someone.

I'd been dating a guy for about six months, and Hobbs was dating another soldier's sister. I wasn't sure how long they'd been together, but I got the vibe that he wasn't that into her since he was so flirtatious with me. He also didn't talk about her. The difficult part was that Hobbs was good friends with his girlfriend's brother, who was in our platoon. They'd known each other for years and were from the same area back home.

I was getting to know my battle buddies and enjoying their personalities. Time spent chatting it up with them was far more exciting than the packing, training, and prepping of our trucks that our days were consumed with. As Christmastime approached, we found out that we were going to be getting a quick leave pass and would get to go home to be with our families.

I was so pumped to be returning to my family. I knew it would be a short visit, and I had no idea what was coming in the future. I did know that I wanted to savor these moments and enjoy my family and friends. Who knew when I would see them again, or ... if I ever would? Those thoughts were hard to swallow, but they were also impossible to ignore.

On my leave, I spent some time with my boyfriend, and things already felt so strange. I'd been gone only three weeks, and I felt like a different person in some ways. It made me somewhat anxious to hang out with him, but I was too uncomfortable to be honest and talk to him about how I was feeling.

Before going to eat on the day we got to visit, I was sitting on his friend's couch putting on my boots when shit suddenly got real.

Moving to the ground and getting on one knee, he said, "I want you to know that I will be here when you get back. Will you marry me?"

With every ounce of doubt creeping into my mind and body, I responded, "Yes." *Did that just come out of my mouth? What the heck just happened? Crap! I'm engaged?*

I knew immediately it was wrong to say yes, but I panicked and felt trapped. This wasn't supposed to happen. What if I had said no? Not sure, but now I knew what happened when you were too chickenshit to be honest.

"Are you going to call your parents?" he asked me excitedly with a smile of anticipation and expectation on his face.

Trying to hide my feelings of instant regret and shock, I faked a smile and called home. My boyfriend—or *freaking fiancé*, I should say—was staring at me, looking for me to be something I was not. I could tell from my mom's tone that she was expecting that from me too. I mean, I was engaged for goodness' sake. That should have been something to celebrate, but she could clearly see right through me. My performance wasn't very impressive, but my mom managed to go along with it. I think she knew it wasn't the right time to question my doubt since he was standing right by me, waiting for some display of overwhelming happiness. My stepdad, Mike, was also on the phone, and I could tell he saw right through it too. I rushed through the call with the excuse that we were headed to eat, and my parents ended it with an awkward congratulations. I was so grateful to get off the phone. That definitely wasn't a proud moment.

My birth father also made his way from Arizona to come spend some time with me before my deployment. This was certainly unexpected since he'd visited me only once in my childhood—well, as far as I could remember. It was a nice visit. He was in a different place in life, and I got to see that before I departed to a combat zone. I finished my leave with my family and friends.

The day came when I had to report back. My mother, birth father, and grandmother drove me back to the unit. My stepdad was not a fan of goodbyes, and I couldn't blame him. This was not a fun goodbye, and I knew it was too much for him to watch any longer than he had to. Goodbye was not what any of us wanted to say.

As we drove, my mom was so pissed off at me. I had stayed out late with friends, my phone died, and she was left worried sick. She's kind of a worry wart, but I don't blame her. I felt bad that my phone died, and it was the last night I was home. She was about to start a whole year of worrying about me. I certainly didn't need to initiate that worry any earlier than expected. Holy cow was she mad!

Meanwhile, when my phone was dead, I was having a long-needed conversation with an ex-boyfriend. He was not just an ex-boyfriend though. Yes, he was my ex. However, he was my first love. I had the opportunity that night to tell him about my regret of my actions and the pain I caused him. He may not even know it, but I spent the night before my fifteen-month deployment apologizing to him.

Unfortunately, during this time, I had no idea that my phone died. My mother was trying to contact me. I was supposed to report to my unit the following morning.

She was freaking out, and I had no idea. I was trying to make some sort of amends for my not-so-proud moments. I returned home and my mother was flaming mad. We loaded up in the car for a forty-minute car ride lecture. I left my momma worrying that night. I had no idea. I did not even realize my phone died.

Even if I did, would I have done anything different? I was headed to a combat zone. I did not realize what that meant, but I knew things were about to change.

After crying my eyes out saying goodbye to my family, I gave my mother one last hug. "Don't you ever do that to me again!" she demanded. I heard her trying to hold back the same release of sadness that I was feeling. I hugged her so tight; I didn't want to let her go. What would I do without my momma just a phone call away? It would be a long time before I was in that embrace again. As I walked to the bus, I looked back at my momma waving, and my heart broke. I had no idea what the year would bring. I had no idea how it would change me forever.

Time to report back to duty ... engaged ... wearing a ring. A ring that I was hiding. Why? Why would I hide it? I wasn't cheating on him. It was just—I knew I wasn't doing the right thing, and I certainly wasn't proud of it. Standing in first formation back to report and take attendance, I felt embarrassed. I nervously tried to hide my ring which was hard to do when you were expected to stand so closely in formation with your hands exposed for all to see. Hiding the ring clearly didn't work. I was busted right away, and some heifer called me out. "Is that a ring? Are you engaged? Congratulations," she announced for all to hear.

Oh yay, just what I wanted! Attention for having a ring on that I instantly regretted. *Please, someone dismiss us fast so I can go to my cot and bury my face.*

#Blessed. Blessed to have a curfew expectation.

The end of December came, and we loaded up in our five-ton trucks, tractor trailers, and a few Humvees. We headed out to the next step in our deployment to Fort McCoy, Wisconsin. There we prepped our trucks, trained for what to expect on convoys, such as small arms fire (people shooting at you) or bombs and mines found on the side of the road.

We finished our training and spent another month in the freezing cold temperatures of Fort McCoy as we waited for our trucks to travel by barge to Kuwait.

With nothing to do, Fort McCoy was a complete shit show for that last month prior to shipping. What do you expect with one hundred sixty people removed from their lives and family waiting to fly to a combat zone? Yes, whatever you are imagining, it probably happened.

Don't get me wrong, our unit's reputation preceded us. Our first sergeant and many others in our unit were squared away leaders. Of course, you have those that are not. We trained and got the job done, then went on R & R on a nightly basis. Brutal at times, but we were surviving, or at least, we thought so.

Bonds were built. Some of us grew a bit, others were stuck in denial. But many of us learned about one another. We had grown to care and depend on one another even before the worst that was yet to come. This is what I think set our unit apart from others. We went deep. We were mostly just a bunch of small-town guardsmen, many of us in our twenties and thirties with a sprinkle of veterans amongst our ranks. All of us just trying to serve our country, or whatever reason that got each of us there.

During our time at Fort McCoy, I ran my sweet game on Ol' Hobbs. We enjoyed each other's company, or at least I thought so. It's not like he ever came over to my barracks to see me. That was a bit more frowned upon, dudes going to the female barracks.

As I started to fall quickly in love with Hobbs, the more disconnected I felt from the life I was living on the home front. Hobbs and I rarely spent time alone. We learned more about one another, but it was limited because you couldn't have personal conversations with everyone listening. We all played a lot of cards. I taught Hobbs how to shuffle cards, and he taught me to find humor in anything. We got to know one another in the brief evenings or moments we had together.

5

THE PAIN CUTS DEEP

JEN:

FINALLY, a weekend with some down time. My battle buddies and I froze our butts off as we walked to the laundry facility carrying our bags of laundry. Even though the ice on the sidewalks was potentially dangerous, we couldn't help but test its accessibility. Seeing how much you could slide as you walked was an activity you had to test out anytime you left the barracks.

The air was so cold it froze my nose and cheeks, yet the laughter kept me warm, not to mention the exercise from hauling the laundry bags. We reached the laundry facility which was a small building that resembled an older post office building. I was immediately grateful for the warmth that embraced me upon our entry. A laundromat area, vending machines, and a room with pay phones—talk about a luxury!

My battles, Cawvey and Marisa, and I made small talk after we started our laundry. I brought up my feelings, or lack thereof, about my new fiancé. They were clearly already aware of how much I regretted the short engagement I had ignorantly agreed to. They had also already witnessed the crush I had on the Ol' Hobbs. They coached me through what I wanted and needed to do: break up with my fiancé.

After much laughter, Cawvey and Marisa helped me compose a breakup script. It included things to say and what *not* to say. I knew it was petty and childish. But man, it was a stellar plan, and I knew they were supporting me the best they could. Not sure why I was so scared. I was hundreds of miles away from this guy and might never have to see him again. So, why the fear?

They prepped me and coached me on the breakup script. He was understanding and made it easier than I expected. Although he'd known me only about six months, he knew I wasn't completely twisted. Also, let's be honest—this was no long-lost love. I mean, I felt bad, but I knew I was doing the right thing, unlike my impulsive reaction to say yes to his proposal back in December.

The rest was history. A history that was written so beautifully, yet so tragically. In the following fourteen months, I and the members of the 1544th, including Ol' Hobbs, would live together, love together, and struggle together. We would lose together, cry together, and grow together. The struggle was real. The struggle *is* real and continues. I believe the struggle is what makes us who we are today and can make us stronger if we allow it to.

We tried to make the most of our days stuck at Fort McCoy. Cawvey loved to prank others, and since I do as well, we made quite the team. One day we hid our battle buddy Spence's rifle under one of our mattresses. We then got the first sergeant to play along. He called Spence to his office, and she flipped because she couldn't find her rifle to carry with her.

She reported to the office without her rifle and came back bawling. We felt awful that it got that serious. We pulled it out and let her know it was just a prank and that we had the first sergeant in on it. She was pissed and not very forgiving. Like I said, we were making the most of our time there, but sometimes it came at a cost. Sorry Spence.

After a month at Fort McCoy, we completed our training. Then we just reported daily to formation for accountability at 0800 hours. We females figured out how not to go through the hassle of putting on every piece of our uniform for morning formation. Instead, we figured out how to get more shut-eye by putting on boots, pants, and our winter GORE-TEX jackets over the shirts we wore to bed rather than putting on a fresh brown T-shirt accompanied with the top of our BDUs. Work smarter, not harder. Ha-ha, not sure that applied here, but it worked for us.

Our days were boring. Some days we went to the morale, welfare, and recreation (MWR) building to use the computers, eat, or just mess around. Most days we made our own entertainment with cases of beer, card games, and delivered food.

The day arrived for us to load up on an airplane to head out for Kuwait. The sky was clear, and the cool crisp breeze felt pleasant to all my senses. Strapped up with our new gear, weapons, and bags, we boarded the plane and packed it in nice and tight.

I took a seat next to Cawvey, our knees squished up from all our gear under our feet. This got uncomfortable real fast on the twenty-hour flight with only two stops, in Germany and Italy. Cawvey was on the struggle bus having to utilize the handy-dandy green barf bags provided in the seat pocket in front of us.

After our arrival, we acclimated to what life in the desert would be like. We brushed our teeth with bottled water and spit it out into the sand of the Kuwait desert. With flashlights strapped around our head and ears, we got the job done. That was the first of many night brushings to come.

Eventually we had travel trailers to brush our teeth in, but then it was just easier to do it on our own. Therefore, a bottle of water was our best friend. A bottle of water to brush our teeth, make food, instant coffee, or just to drink. Bottled water was a blessing. However, they say that you shouldn't leave your bottled water in the sun or heat because it leaches chemicals from the plastic, right? Our bottled water was delivered on pallets and left there until we consumed it.

It was certainly not delicious, but we were grateful for the water.

We spent a month in Kuwait waiting for our trucks to arrive. Training continued, boredom led our days, and even walking to chow seemed like a defeating task at times. The chow hall was a quarter mile away. The sinking Kuwait sand made it quite a workout just to go catch a meal. You basically burned the same number of calories on the challenging walk as in the meal itself.

The wind sometimes added to the obstacle. On windy days, the sand snuck into the craziest places even when you had every inch of your body covered up. The worst was getting sand in your eyes. Sometimes, we skipped a meal and ate snacks instead to avoid the trek to chow.

Our lives were contained to the tents they provided our units to live in. Outside of that, we didn't have much. You had your battle buddies that you talked to and your devices that you came with, whether that was a DVD player or a coloring book.

Our trucks finally arrived at port, and we convoyed to secure them. We were already aware that we would be heading north near Baghdad, Iraq. At a platoon meeting one night, our platoon sergeant changed his tone, serious and tinged with melancholy.

"It is likely that not all of us will make it home," he said with sincerity as he looked around at us. The gravity of his honesty cut like a knife. I looked around at all those around me. Dumbfounded, we all just listened and inhaled what was being said.

Prior to rolling out of Kuwait, we spent a few days adding some makeshift protection onto our trucks. We mounted welded pieces of metal that covered the doors of the bed of the trucks, and we enhanced the turrets on top. We built rectangular boxes made of wood with sandbags inside to attempt some sort of barrier for the gunners that would be in each of our turrets.

March 16, 2004, we arrived at Log Base Seitz in a few fleets. Log Base Seitz is positioned between the Baghdad International Airport and about 1500 meters from Abu Ghraib. We parked our trucks and grabbed our gear. We were led to two large, towering tin buildings that stood taller than all the buildings on the base. The buildings were filled with old metal bunks with mattresses that looked about twenty years old. We bunked down for the night, most of us on cots because there weren't enough bunks.

The next day, St. Patrick's Day, just before our first training on mortar attacks, we received an incoming mortar attack. Although we'd never been through one, it was obvious this was an attack. We reacted immediately. Everyone hit the ground as we heard explosions so loud, they shook the earth below us.

They continued to fall, and when it sounded as though the rounds had stopped, I climbed to my feet and followed the crowd of soldiers running toward the exit. Running outside, turning the corner to head toward the underground bunkers, I heard more explosions. On the other side of the barriers, I could see dust in the sky from the impact of the mortars. I panicked, but others running with and around me did not drop to the ground again, so I didn't either. I hauled ass to the designated first platoon bunker. Not sure why they were already designated since we hadn't been trained yet to know what the hell a mortar attack was or what to do in case of one, but I leapt over the entrance of three underground bunkers before I got to the one I thought I was supposed to go to for accountability. This, I realized, wasn't the best decision, and it would be the last time I was ever picky about a bunker.

Rushing into the crowded bunker, I was panting and trying to catch my breath as I heard more mortars falling around us, but I couldn't see much. The looks on all our faces were unforgettable. Wide-eyed and terrified, our boots were soaking in five inches of sitting water as we listened for the mortars to stop. Finally, no more fell, and we could finally exhale.

"Holy shit, that was crazy," someone said.

This was the first time most of us had experienced a wartime situation, and we were feeling several emotions. We were still in shock, but our adrenaline was so high that we were all talking about what our perspectives were when the attack started and what we were doing. Some stories were funny since some people were in the middle of using the restroom or getting dressed. There was a little laughter in the bunker, but mostly shock and conversations attempting to process what the hell just happened. Finally, we got the all clear and climbed out one by one with sopping feet and hearts beating out of our chests. We reported to accountability, and this ... this was the first time that I would see the faces of trauma.

The first sergeant took roll call. He debriefed us the best he could on what had just transpired. He let us know that some soldiers in our unit had been medevacked out, and he would keep us updated. Later that day, he called formation again to deliver the shitty news. The heart-wrenching, shitty news that we lost our first soldier that day. Sergeant Ivory Phipps lost his life when he was hit by shrapnel from a mortar. As much as the combat life savers tried, the injuries were too extensive, and we felt the pain of losing a fallen comrade within just twenty-four hours of being on Log Base Seitz, aka Mortaritaville. Unfortunately, it wouldn't be the last time we felt that excruciating pain.

After March 17th, we quickly learned how things worked. We started our convoy missions, transporting troops and escorting some convoys to provide more gun security. We also got put on the mail routes to convoy around Iraq and deliver mail to the bases. We didn't carry the mail in our trucks. We worked with KBR drivers, contracted American civilians, some of which were military Veterans. They drove semis to haul CONEX boxes, a type of shipping container, full of mail.

As gun security, we spaced our trucks out in these convoys to provide gun support, loaded with fire power in case the convoy was attacked. The problem was, most attacks made against our convoys came in the form of IEDs (improvised explosive devices). These were more difficult to identify as opposed to small arms fire or even rocket-propelled grenades (RPGs). At least with those, you could usually see where they were coming from.

May 23, 2004, one of our first platoon convoys was attacked with small arms fire when a vehicle on the side of the road, loaded with explosives, detonated. We lost another kind soul that day, Jeremy Ridlen. Our unit had already experienced trauma, and this loss was another blow to my platoon. We were a family, but the pain we felt wouldn't come close to the pain that another soldier in our unit would endure for a lifetime—Jeremy's twin brother was also in our unit. He lost his other half that day. That pain, I can only imagine, is unspeakable.

We had been "in country" for only a few months, and we had already endured the pain of two soldiers killed in action (KIA). Things didn't get any easier as the months passed. Convoys were hit, people were injured but fortunately survived multiple attacks. Our base continued to receive frequent mortar attacks. Bunkers improved as cement barriers were brought into our base. We worked together to make so many damn sandbags and added them to make secured bunkers.

One day as we were bagging what seemed like a ridiculous amount of sandbags, someone asked me sarcastically, "Hey Buff, where's Hobbs?" They knew darn well where he was. He was in the "good ol' boys" system, so no one was going to say anything to him about not coming out to help with the platoon sandbagging.

"Hey Buff, where's Cawvey?" This time it was Sergeant Arturo asking.

"Um, I'm not sure," I said, knowing very well that she was asleep in the barracks. She was like Hobbs—they were skilled in doing their own thing.

"Well, go find her and tell her to get out here and sandbag," he ordered.

Fine with me. I caught a break from shoveling sand in the 120-degree weather. I walked into the barracks where there was at least some airflow from the shade and a few fans. *Ah, feels like a breath of fresh air.* Those tin buildings were far from a breath of fresh air, but I was appreciative of them.

I walked up to Cawvey's bunk where I saw her fast asleep.

"Psst. Hey. Hey, Cawvey, wake up," I said as I nudged her.

"What?" she questioned with irritation.

"Sergeant Arturo sent me in to get you for sandbagging detail," I passed on the lame information to her.

"Tell them you couldn't wake me up," she tiredly responded and rolled over.

"Will do! Sleep tight!" I said matter-of-factly and headed back to deliver the message.

Mission accomplished, Cawvey caught up on some sleep. She was such a boss babe.

Our platoons were divided into different convoy teams. First platoon had three teams. One day I was put on a mission to transport troops from one base to another. Since the beds of our trucks would be filled with troops, we were assigned gun security provided by another gun security team consisting mostly of military police.

Prior to rolling out on the convoy, I stood in a large group that circled around the convoy commander. He briefed us on the mission and then the craziest thing happened to me. I glanced around at the soldiers of this gun security team, and I caught sight of a sergeant directly across from me in the circle, smiling and shaking his head.

I instantly noticed that it was Drill Sergeant Jeanz from my basic training. Oh my God! I never thought I'd see him again. I struggled not to let out a laugh, and when the convoy commander finished, I headed over to Sergeant First Class Jeanz. So happy to see a familiar face, I enjoyed a quick conversation with him prior to the convoy. Luckily, when we got to our destination, I was able to catch up with him a little bit longer. It was so bizarre to cross paths in a combat zone with someone who was such a role model to me, and he probably didn't even know it.

6

DEUCES, IRAQ!

Hobbs:

In the sweltering heat of Iraq, we ran missions providing gun security for KBR drivers. Sometimes, if we were going on a less dangerous route, I handed over my M16 to one of the KBR drivers to use. They were not allowed to carry weapons, so I shared when I could. However, the times when we were going into the Green Zone or somewhere where buildings would be close or on routes that we knew were more dangerous, I preferred to have it with me.

When I wasn't on the road, I spent a lot of time playing Halo on the PlayStation with the guys at the barracks. My little spitfire, Buff, came over to visit when she could. Sometimes we watched a movie together.

On our base, we had a small shop where the Iraqi civilians sold various items including bootlegged movies. Score! We had access to so many movies, many of which weren't released on video yet. Of course, the quality was trash, but it was entertainment, nonetheless.

One day as Shaun and I were walking back from the shop, we chatted it up.

"I wonder if you can see a mortar as it falls," Shaun said.

"Good question. I wonder if they are too fast to identify," I replied.

Just as I finished my sentence, it was like those bastards heard me, and mortars fell all around us. "Holy shit, get down," he said, but I was already down. We were awkwardly laughing as they fell, even though we were both a bit scared. The mortars stopped. We climbed to our feet, and walked back to the barracks, alive and laughing at the intense moment we had just shared.

CLOSE TO MY TWENTY-FIFTH BIRTHDAY, my unit told me that the two-week leave I had requested at the beginning of deployment was coming up. I remembered that months ago, at the beginning of our deployment, each of us had the opportunity to request what date we would prefer for our two-week leave during the deployment. After it was said and done, it was one of those things that was forgotten. Sure, it was what you requested, but you certainly weren't banking on it. At least I wasn't.

You got so wrapped up in the now and where you were, you didn't waste your time waiting to return home for two weeks. Home seemed like a faraway land you wouldn't see for a long, long time. Time passed, phone calls were rare, and the existence around you was all you had. Your new normal was foreign to you at first, but soon became routine. Sure, it was far more unpredictable than your previous civilian life, but routine, nonetheless.

Suddenly, I was headed to the home front. Fortunately, I wasn't alone. Another battle buddy of mine, Johns, was also headed home for her leave. I couldn't even believe it. I was beyond pumped but couldn't ignore the complicated feelings that came with the opportunity to head home. I was excited to get back to American soil, but I had to leave my friends and unit behind ... *in a combat zone.*

I understood that the Army wanted people to have that time to go home and be with their family and friends. But the feelings that came with it—they were not something that people should experience. Leave may be beneficial for others, but for me, it wasn't good.

I was headed back home, a place that hadn't been home in nine months. I saw the shape of the land of Iraq grow smaller out my airplane window. I only imagined that Johns felt the same overwhelming feelings I felt at the airport and during the processing. I felt completely out of place. I wasn't sure what I was going to do when I got home, but I knew that I needed to get away from all those crowds of strangers.

It felt peculiar to walk through a crowded airport coming from a combat zone. I felt unprotected, a bit defenseless, and unknown bags of cargo were everywhere. I was dissecting the movements of everyone and scanning their presence.

As one sketchy-looking guy walked away from his bag on the ground, my mind left my body. All I could think about were our convoys in Iraq, attacks, and makeshift bombs, improvised devices that the enemies created and disguised to fool us.

I will not be complacent! My pulse kicked into overdrive, and I couldn't even hear Johns talking to me. When I saw the man pick up his bag and walk away, a sense of relief came over me. It was then I realized that Johns was trying to get my attention.

"Hobbs! Hobbs! The exit is this way. Let's go. Move your

ass, I want to get home," she demanded with a smile, but I could tell she felt anxious and defenseless as well. I snapped out of it and moved with a purpose—a purpose to get the hell out of there!

Overseas, I was a gunner on our convoys. My job was to ride in the bed of our trucks and continuously scan 360 degrees as we maneuvered through foreign territory. I stood in a gun box welded together with sheets of metal. My M16 stayed with me, but my main weapon was the 50 caliber, what we referred to as a 50 cal. I was trained to look out for items lying around that could be used to build an IED, which was basically anything those dirty bastards could get their hands on.

With determination, we made it to the exit. Instant feelings of relief came over me. The strange thing was, it wasn't because we were finally home, but rather because we had just escaped the chaos in this melting pot of sketchy-ass people.

It was hard to find pure joy or pleasure in the days of my leave. I got to see my family, though, which was good. It was also rather confusing. It was hard to separate one life from another. One day you were constantly protecting yourself and your people from enemy attacks, and the next you were home facing so many decisions. Decisions I hadn't made in almost a year.

"Do you want to play the PlayStation or go out to eat?"

"What do you want to eat?"

"Want to go fishing?"

"Want something to drink? I bet you could use a beer."

The stimulation of so many people and decisions was paralyzing. I was puzzled, thinking, *Hell no, I don't want to go out to eat. You mean I get a choice on what to eat?* So many choices, I didn't even know what I wanted. I wasn't sure I even knew how to fish anymore. *Hell yeah, I need a beer.*

Leave was a blur, but I did get to spend an evening fishing

with my stepdad and enjoying one of my favorite pastimes. As we were fishing at a small rearing pond, some bad weather rolled in. We later discovered it was a tornado approaching nearby. It was too far in the distance to see, and we barely got sprinkled on. The clouds looked so dark, and we saw lightning in the distance. We lost signals on our phones, but we said screw it and continued casting for more catfish.

We laughed and drank all night. I was grateful he didn't ask me a bunch of questions related to the deployment. As a matter of fact, people didn't really do that when I was home—well, at least not those closest to me. Don't get me wrong, things blurred together, especially with all the confusing events that happened along the way. But I don't remember having to face the reality of what was happening on the other side of the world, which was weird. So, I just went with it.

The next morning as we pulled out the boat, still unaware of the severe weather from the evening before—we survived so it didn't faze us—we started to put the fish baskets in the boat with last night's catch.

"Aren't these channel cats?" I asked.

"Yeah," he replied with confidence and pleasure.

I laughed and pointed over to the sign, "Well that sign says there is a limit of six." We both laughed, a bit panicked.

"Well let's get the hell out of here!" my stepdad said nervously.

I enjoyed the rest of my leave hanging out with friends and spending too much time at the bar. I made a quick visit to see my dad and extended family in Kentucky. It was nice to be home, but the strange feelings of displacement and guilt that came with it outweighed the enjoyment.

. . .

"I'M GOING TO TASE YOU!" An unfamiliar voice broke into my consciousness.

Tase me? Ha-ha. What? What the hell is going on?

The words were loud and clear, which was super strange since I had no recollection of what led up to the moments prior to hearing those words. One minute I was celebrating my last night on the home soil, then boom, real life hit me like a ton of bricks, and I realized what I had gotten myself into.

I was rolling around in the dirt with another person. I struggled to wrestle out of their grip. At that very moment, through the darkness of the night, I noticed flashing emergency lights out of the corner of my eye. I instantly went limp and gave in to the fight against this unknown silhouette as I realized the person I was wrestling was in uniform.

Ah shit. Good thing I went limp when I heard his threat of tasing me because my ass was wrestling a cop! The unknown silhouette *was a cop!* I gained consciousness and realized I was out in a cornfield a good distance from my car.

What the hell? Oh, boy! What happened?

I started to remember how I enjoyed a few too many tequila shots at the bar prior to driving home. I agreed to take his Breathalyzer. What was the point in refusing when I could hardly stand? Next thing I knew, I was in the back of his squad car, knees squished up, hand cuffs so tight I had to lean to the side.

What just happened? "Hey, sorry about all that back there," I offered on the ride to the station. He didn't say anything and honestly, I didn't expect him to. I felt bad though.

During questioning at the station, they asked me about my employment.

"Well currently, I am a 50-cal gunner for the Army in Iraq." They were a bit taken aback when I told them I had been in Iraq the last six months, and I was only home on leave.

"I'm supposed to be at the airport at 1:00 p.m. tomorrow," I stated nonchalantly.

They booked me and did what they needed to do but never put me in a jumpsuit or in a cell. The same arresting officer drove me home. This time he allowed me to ride in the passenger seat of the squad car. I think they realized what they were dealing with—a soldier home from a combat zone, getting blasted on the last night before his return. Not a pretty sight, nor anything to encourage and dismiss, but they did what they felt they needed to do and released me. The officer and I talked the whole way back to my house. When we arrived at my house, we got out of the car and continued talking for about ten more minutes. He shook my hand, told me good luck, and said goodbye before he left.

Charged with a DUI after falling asleep on the side of the road and wrestling the cop, I was now back home, packed and loaded up to return to Iraq to join my unit. Dear God! I was still hammered. They just let me go, and they knew I was going to be driving to the airport soon. *Well, damn, thank you. Now what? Oh yeah, back to reality.* I wasn't even sure what that was anymore.

At the airport, I looked for Johns. It was a relief and comfort to see a familiar face from the life I lived prior to the shit show I just put myself through. The reality I had neglected for a few weeks reunited quickly with my being. A complete out-of-body experience, dazed and confused, I felt like I was in a dream. Johns and I walked to the counter to check in.

"Well, you are a day early folks. You are welcome to stay. We will put you up in a hotel for the night, and you can catch your plane tomorrow. Unless you'd prefer to go today," the flight representative broke the unexpected news to us, as I was still trying to gain my composure and grasp the moment in time. I was just in the backseat of a cop car early this morning with fresh DUI charges, and now I was a day early to go back to Iraq. Talk about karma!

Hmm, should we stay and enjoy one more night out?

A few hours later, I was strapped into my seatbelt and listening to the flight attendant's safety briefing on masks and emergency exits, sounding more like the adults from the Charlie Brown cartoon, "Wah wah wah wah." I was headed back to Iraq a day early. Of course, we didn't choose to stay another night. That time of rest was over. Ha-ha, okay, okay, *rest* wouldn't be the word to describe that mess. But we had already been anticipating our return, and there was no getting around that. There was nothing that would be enjoyable at that point that would make us comfortable. Nothing. Time to return to the combat zone. I hoped I had everything I needed. That was a legitimate concern since I seemed to have lost myself and my identity in just a few weeks. I haven't felt comfortable in my skin in this place I used to call home.

7

ROCKED AT MORTARITAVILLE

JEN:

WE TRIED to make the most of our days. We had to. There was no other choice unless you wanted to live in a depressed state—totally not living.

One early morning after a late-night mission, Cawvey and I decided to take a walk around the base near the motor pool where we parked our trucks. All was calm and the morning sunrise was delightful until shit hit the fan.

We looked at each other when we thought we heard the same *floomp* sound. That was the sound of a mortar round launching from a tube. Typically, we didn't hear them. On that calm morning, we did. We didn't have even a second to react before the rounds started falling near us.

Only ten feet from the entrance of a bunker, we took our chances and ran like hell. We made it! Mortar rounds were still showering all around our bunker. They were so close we heard the shrapnel pieces tinking off the vehicles.

"Holy shit that was close," Cawvey said, panting with shock.

"No doubt! Those bastards are up early. Shouldn't they be praying or something?" I replied, trying to catch my breath.

This was unlike any other morning. Most mornings the loud prayer music that belted out of the speakers all over the city of Abu Ghraib was loud and clear at Mortaritaville. Not today though. They were seeking blood, not prayer.

The mortar rounds stopped falling, and Cawvey and I spent what seemed like a few hours in the bunker before we got the all clear. Since we were at a bunker in the motor pool, we were one of the last ones to be checked on and given the all clear. We had plenty of time to chat and laugh.

About ten minutes after the mortar shower, our hearts were still racing, and the adrenaline was still pumping when we heard a helicopter flying nearby.

It got closer.

Then even closer.

Closer, closer ... it was about to crash into us!

From a sitting position, Cawvey pushed me to the ground and lay on top of me. Literally lay on top of me! As the helicopter passed by, relief came over us as we acknowledged we were still alive.

"Dude, you just tried to save my life," I said laughing, but I felt so many more emotions. *I love this bitch!*

"I thought that shit was going to crash into us," she replied with eyes wide.

I'll never forget that morning. Cawvey was going to lay down her life to protect me. I know she would have done it for anyone.

She knew I had her back too! I always would. In the middle of the night one night, she came into my cubicle and woke me up. I was passed out sleeping.

"Psst, Buff ... Buff ... wake up. Can you help me?" I quickly opened my eyes, trying to gain my composure and figure out what was going on.

That was when I saw Cawvey standing by my bunk. "Hey, can you help me sneak this dude out of the barracks?"

Without asking any questions or hesitating, I jumped from my top bunk. I followed her and headed for the exit door to be a lookout. After assessing the situation, I signaled a thumbs up to her and motioned for them to move. As the male passed by me, I realized I had no idea who it was.

I spent the next few hours of the early morning laughing and chatting with Cawvey. She told me that the man was someone she had met before—this time, it was a birthday present to herself. Seemed legitimate. *Cawvey, you little sneaky hustler, you!*

Hobbs was gone on his two-week leave. I hoped he was having fun, but I sure missed him. It was comforting to know he was safer on the home front. That was what I wanted to think, but he had told me some crazy stories about his bachelor life. I hoped he wouldn't revert to his old ways and enjoy himself too much.

The sun shone brightly, and it was a beautiful day. I walked to the male barracks for a platoon meeting. The females were no longer living over with the males at our original barracks. After some scandalous fraternization-related issues, all the females on the entire post were moved to reside in the same large tin building. The building was about four hundred meters from the main barracks. It wasn't a straight shot either. We couldn't see them, and they couldn't see us since the shower trailers and chow hall were between us and them.

Just before I reached the barracks for the meeting, I noticed someone step out of the Porta-Potty. Fresh new buzz cut, fresh white tennis shoes. Hobbs was back and looking fly as hell in new shoes!

"Oh my God, you're back!" I said as I ran up to give him a hug.

He smiled that killer smile and told me that he'd missed me. I was so pumped! My heart settled a bit from the anxiety that I'd carried with me during his absence. *Oh, my goodness! I love this human being! Hobbs is back!*

Having him back in a combat zone was a comfort for me, and I thought he seemed to have stronger feelings for me. He embraced me longer with those tight bear hugs. We both understood that our relationship was growing at an exponential speed with deep, intense emotions. We didn't have to speak of it. We both felt it. We may not have acknowledged it verbally for a long time, but we were both conscious of how it felt. It was like another shield of comfort in this combat zone.

I purposely visited the male barracks often so I could have an excuse to see Hobbs. He was usually occupied playing games of Halo with his battle buddies. Sometimes watching movies together, or just sleeping. There's not much to do in a combat zone.

Before his visit home, I felt as though I annoyed him and the dudes, since you don't just roll up during intense battles on Halo talking some girly garbage. However, there was certainly a clear change in his demeanor since he had returned. He seemed more passionate and more grateful for our relationship.

Now, understand when I say *passionate*, for Hobbs, I'm not talking about any sort of exceptional displays of public feelings. I didn't need that, and being on active duty status, that was not acceptable by the standards. So, that had never been my expectation. Don't get me wrong, sometimes I could be high-maintenance.

What was unexpected was his obvious verbal and

nonverbal display of emotions. Tighter, longer hugs. Longer moments looking into my eyes in those personal, calm moments. He is my person. I believe I am also his.

We kept most of our relationship to ourselves and tried not to put it on public display. We were the same rank, E-4 Specialist. Technically we couldn't be punished for fraternization, or at least I didn't think so. We were not married to someone else, nor were we different ranks. It was still frowned upon though, so we kept our business to ourselves as much as we could.

Since it was Hobbs's birthday month, I tried to figure out what I could get him that would mean a lot. I wanted to show him that I listened and that I also cared about what he valued. With my mother's help, I was able to get him a Saint Christopher necklace. His mom had given him one just like it before the deployment, but it broke during the first six months of our deployment. He had worn it every day and hadn't taken it off before it broke. After looking it up to see what it represented, I learned that Saint Christopher was the saint of travelers.

———

Saint Christopher Protection Prayer

"Dear Saint Christopher, protect me today in all my travels along the road's way. Give your warning sign if danger is near so that I may stop while the path is clear. Be at my window and direct me through when the vision blurs from out of the blue. Carry me safely to my destined place, like you carried Christ in your close embrace. Amen."

———

FROM THE MALE BARRACKS, the chow hall was a straight shot about two hundred fifty meters away. Between the chow hall and the male barracks, there was a sand volleyball court where we enjoyed some fun competition with our unit. There was also a small building where chapel services were held and a large sign, like one you might see on vacation, painted in bold letters: "Mortaritaville." A term used for military bases that were often subjected to regular attacks. The term suited our base perfectly. We were a major target for the enemy. Sometimes RPGs, rarely small arms fire, and mostly mortar attacks, around two hundred thirty-five mortar rounds came our way during our deployment.

September 5th, around midday as soldiers were walking to and from chow, devastation came to us as we were attacked with mortars walked in by the enemy. "Walking in" involved popping off one mortar, identifying where it landed, then walking, or moving to get closer each time. Unlike most mortar attacks that we experienced that year, this was far different. The first mortar came in as a direct hit, landing between my unit's two large male barracks. We were not on a high level of alert; therefore, people were not walking around wearing their protective gear.

I was in my cubicle living space in the female barracks about four hundred meters away when the mortar assault started. I was putting on my boots to walk over to chow before the earth-shaking explosion ravaged our base. I hit the floor immediately and recognized the intense closeness of the explosions. It felt like one was about to come through the roof at any time. My body tensed up as I prayed fiercely.

Oh, Dear Lord, make it stop. Please Lord make it stop!

After about six mortar explosions and a long pause, I frantically climbed to my feet, grabbed my weapon, and ran. The crowd of females tried to escape out one small single-door exit from our building. As we all ran out, some went left, some went right. There was a bunker on each side of the building. I don't know why, but our unit females typically retreated to the same one.

We spent more time in the bunker than we would have liked. But it felt safer when we were outside chatting and hanging out. This bunker had become familiar to us. This was the same bunker I'd spent a morning laughing with Cawvey in complete relief as we reenacted our survival from a fierce morning mortar attack. I had memories in this bunker, but this would be one of the worst.

We knew it was a bad attack. Everyone was shaken and concerned beyond belief. That was our family over there! Before they moved us females, we used to be in the same bunkers with them during mortar attacks. I felt better being with them during those times. Now we were together in a bunker with females from other units we didn't even know.

Out one of the entrances to the bunker, we saw medevacs driving from the direction of our main barracks to the troop medical clinic. I stood there in complete dismay as the fear bled through my body. *What is happening?*

Just then, a sergeant from another company, whom we'd never really interacted with, entered our bunker. She had walked over from the other bunker. She questioned, "Anyone from the 1544th in here?"

Like a bunch of deer in headlights, we stared at her, nodding, and some managed to answer her. I was thinking, *Ugh ... duh bitch. You know damn well that ninety percent of the females in here are from the 1544th.*

"Yes," a few of our females replied.

"Well, y'all better start praying. Your unit has been hit hard."

Terrified and shaken with disbelief, we looked around at one another. We grabbed hands and prayed.

Hooray Sergeant Lame Ass! Way to lead, moron. Instead of providing us with the comfort we needed during such a devastating experience, she stole what little hope we were clinging to.

About an hour passed and we still hadn't received the all clear signal yet. A few of us slowly started making our way out of one of the bunker entrances to see daylight. A fellow 1544th battle buddy walked by, clearly involved in the sweep of the base after the mortar attack. Sweeps were done to check on the different impact spots, as well as to look for unexploded mortars.

One of our females asked him how the status was as he hustled past, clearly agitated. The horror on his face was obvious and something I've never forgotten. "It's bad. It's real bad," he said as he continued past us.

Standing there stunned, we all froze in time for a moment, unable to move or breathe. Then we did the only thing some of us knew to do—we kept praying. Prayer and each other was all we had at that moment.

Oh shit. What is that sound? Oh God, I know that's a helicopter. I just know it.

As the sound got closer and louder, the medevac helicopter came into sight.

What in the actual fuck is going on? Let us out of here. We need to get to our unit. Dear Lord, let them be okay. Please Lord!

What seemed like a lifetime later, we finally received the all clear and were released from the bunkers. Finally! We grabbed our weapons and exited frantically. We ran inside to grab our protective gear. I threw my Kevlar on my head, wrapped my flak jacket around my chest, and grabbed my weapon.

Fearful of the unknown, many of us ran together to our main barracks. Once the barracks were in sight, we slowed down and walked with a purpose. At first, nothing seemed obviously out of place. People were walking around. Some soldiers were sweeping the sidewalks. I saw the brooms kicking up tons of dust from the dirt. *Why would they be sweeping right now?* I noticed that they were taking the dirt and pushing it *onto* the sidewalk. Then it dawned on me. They were covering up the blood they tried to clean.

We slowly gathered into formation. Something wasn't right. Nothing was right. I saw it in so many of the faces around me. Faces that were no longer unfamiliar and new to me. I knew their faces, their demeanors, their nonverbal body language. I knew something was not right.

Sadly, I was right. Things were a blur after formation, but then later that day we were called into the chow hall. Oh God. We knew what that meant. It wasn't good.

We entered the chow hall in silence and stared in fear about what we would hear.

"Today we lost Shawna Morrison and Charles Lamb," someone said. I was numb and couldn't comprehend what was going on. Then, a gut-wrenching wail of sorrow escaped from the mouth of one of Lamb's best friends. Sorrow hit like a blast to the soul.

The enemy rocked us that day, walking in the mortars starting at a common gathering area between the two main barracks of our unit members, including the tactical operations center (TOC) where our administration team ran operations out of. They hit the heart of our unit, then walked in more mortars extending between our main barracks and the chow hall, covering approximately three hundred meters.

Our unit lost two soldiers, KIA, that day, and approximately twenty others were injured from the attack. The injuries were so deep and so vast that I can't express the effect on our unit. It was life-changing, and the effects on our members are something I can't put into words. The effects are endless.

To say that war leaves battle wounds is an understatement. Yes, it does, both physical and emotional battle wounds, but there is so much more. There is so much more pain and suffering that comes in the years that follow the combat zone. But more importantly, there is so much growth that can come from that unrelenting pain and trauma. "Struggle can bring profound gifts." (Falke and Goldberg 2018). This is true.

8

OCTOBER 6TH, 2004

JEN:

As WE CONTINUED our missions and wrestled with the all-consuming feelings of trauma that struck our unit just a short month ago, we moved into the month of October. Trying to stay positive and focused on our primary mission, the taste of home starts to creep in. *When will this be over?*

On the 6th of October, Hobbs and his gun team were loading up around dinner time, preparing to roll out for their night mission. The team was a bit different then it normally was. Some soldiers were swapped out for various reasons. This was the very first mission for one of our first platoon females, Andrea. Some of us not going on the mission were out there helping them pack up and taking pictures prior to their departure. Andrea and Cawvey were besties, along with our battle buddy Willy. We met Willy at the beginning of the deployment. He was originally in a unit out of Chicago and was attached to our unit for the deployment just as Sergeant Phipps was and about a dozen others.

At the beginning of the deployment Andrea and Cawvey were given nicknames at one of our training ranges. Andrea was Number One and Cawvey was Number Two. Cawvey was also known as The Cawvster. Cawvster and Andrea shared a bunk/cubicle area. Since this was Andrea's first mission, Cawvster was adamant on going. She knew Andrea was scared shitless; nevertheless, she really wanted to go on one. She had been holding a vital central radio position on the base for the bulk of the year. Cawvster was not going to let her homie go on her first mission without her.

As they rolled out, I continued to chat with my girl, Bert. She was put on fireguard duty for the evening. This duty involved having to post up inside the TOC. I decided to stick around and keep her company whupping her at card games.

"Call for medevac," I heard one of the sergeants posted up at the computers say.

Did they just say what I think they said? Instantly, Bert and I froze, our playing cards clenched in our grip. Every bone and muscle tightened in our bodies. Thoughts and questions immediately started racing in my head, moving so fast I was unable to process them.

Bert and I sat and watched the tragedy unravel before us. A picture of shock, fear, and utter disbelief, we stared as we saw the two sergeants frantically hustling around. I could tell something was wrong. I saw and felt the stress in the room. Bert and I couldn't take our eyes off trying to figure out *who* they were talking about and *what* was going on.

Young, inexperienced, and fragile to tragedy ... we had no idea what the following hours would bring. We had no idea what the following days and years would bring to us all.

Prior to the call for the medevac, we were outside the

TOC when we heard an enormous explosion in the distance. We could tell it was most likely a roadside bomb somewhere around Fallujah. It was the kind of bomb that shook the earth for miles and sent chills up your spine, knowing "that was a bad one." We thought nothing of it and returned inside to continue with our card game. After living on Mortaritaville for seven months, we'd become educated on the different types of explosions and their distances.

While Bert and I were faking our card game, one of the sergeants called out with urgency, "I need a blood type!" I instantly thought of Hobbs. He was out there! I'd just said goodbye to him when they packed up their trucks. *Oh no, they were headed north. They would pass by Fallujah.*

No way ... not happening ... no way ... no way! They need a blood type. What does that mean? Has somebody lost so much blood that they need a transfusion? What? Who? What? Somebody tell us something!

The core of my body bubbled like magma waiting to explode. Intensity built up, and just then, the base chaplain walked in. We didn't see him often. Only if we attended church service—or when we lost a soldier. In our case, the feeling was far too familiar. We had already lost four amazing human beings. Our battle buddies, yes, but they were also someone's child, parent, sibling, family member, and friend.

It sounds terrible, but at that point, he felt like the Grim Reaper. He walked in at the worst time ever imaginable. He slowly walked toward Bert and me, as we still stared in complete awe and dismay. This strange man that we knew only from situations of loss, sat down at our table. In his blank stare, I saw the sadness in his expression.

What's up with this guy? I couldn't even find the words to greet him with the recognition an officer expects. Breaking the silence, he said, "It's always so hard when we lose someone we love."

Oh, hell no! What is this guy talking about? Is something going on, and we have to hear the awful news from a chaplain we don't even know?

In unison, Bert and I jumped up from our seats and found the nearest first platoon leader so that we could figure out what was going on.

We found one of our squad leaders, Sergeant Arturo. He wiped the sleep out of his eyes, trying to comprehend what Bert and I were saying. We were frantic and a hot mess. We ambushed him with questions. "What happened? It's our platoon, isn't it? Whose truck? We heard it was the last truck in our first platoon convoy. Is that true?"

Tragedy made that ball of sickness and sadness creep into my throat. Sergeant Arturo reassured us calmly and stayed with us. I was sure he withheld some information from us as we tried to pry it from him. He tried to keep us calm as we panicked and dreaded what was to come, or worse ... who wouldn't.

The darkness of the night passed with brutal torture. We continued to pace into the TOC and back out to the bunker where we sat and waited. We received word that a first platoon convoy had been hit, and it was the last truck of the convoy. One soldier was KIA.

Wait a minute ... Hobbs is always in the last truck of his convoy. K-I-what? No, no, no! This is not happening!

Memories flooded my thoughts. The time I first told Hobbs I loved him, we were lying together in his bunk, under the camo netting that allowed a bit of privacy. He knew I meant it, and when he told me he loved me too, I knew our love was deep.

The following hours and early morning dragged on. Our hearts raced, yet we tried to remain calm and not to get kicked out of the TOC. Bert and I had already been warned about needing to stay calm or we would have to leave.

I felt like a mixed bag of psycho, sad, scared, confused, and devastated by emotions that burned through my body. I managed to keep my composure into the wee hours of the morning, waiting for the convoy to return. The saddest hours were yet to come.

A sense of relief came over me when my squad leader, Sergeant Lave, walked into the TOC. It was nice to see another familiar face in the midst of the growing fear. He led me outside to the bunker to chat.

"I do know that it was a first platoon convoy. It was the convoy Hobbs is on," he confirmed. My soul shuddered. Clearly fighting back tears, he explained that he had been informed that one soldier was KIA and that he did not know who it was but did not think that it was him. He did tell me that he thought it was his truck that was hit and that he was most likely injured. My heart sank.

We prayed. We cried. Then prayed some more.

Let's just pause and take a moment to revisit this statement. This shitty-ass, life-altering, unfair, bullshit statement: *One soldier is KIA.*

One friend ... one child ... one battle buddy ... one *American soldier.*

I couldn't leave. I stayed all night waiting for the convoy to return. We still hadn't received any other details. We were left to imagine, wonder, and fear the worst. The night dragged on forever. Bert and I waited on pins and needles.

Hobbs was usually driven by our homegirl, Joy. She was a petite, strong, happy ball of badass. Hobbs preferred her driving and trusted her with his life.

Who was coming back? Who was not? We wouldn't know until they arrived.

We heard the five-ton trucks rolling toward us, the dreadful moment we'd waited for all night. The trucks slowly crept out of the darkness with soldiers walking in front as ground guides. We waited, staring in horror to see who was going to get out of the trucks ... and who would not. I heard myself breathing fast, and I thought my heart would beat out of my chest.

The convoy came to a halt in the darkness about twenty meters away from the TOC where we stood. The trucks turned off and then ... silence. Silhouettes of soldiers dismounted from the trucks. It looked as though they came together in a huddle and then ... that dreadful noise. The heart-wrenching wail broke the silence.

Oh, my God, that was Andrea. Oh shit! No! No! No! No! It can't be! Where's Cawvey? I can't identify her silhouette through the darkness. Ugh, I can't see. Find her! Find her!

The walk back to our female barracks was heart-breaking as we helped carry the girls' gear. Silence so uncomfortable, I could barely breathe. The pain was deep and unrelenting. With barrels of questions flowing through my mind, I remained silent, as it seemed the most appropriate thing to do. I mean, what was there to say at such a horrible time? *Who died?* Yeah ... sounds harsh, right? Of course, your mind is thinking it, but you dare not say it.

Our walk in the starlit sky came to an end as we approached the darkness before our barracks. The horrific, life-changing words choked out of one of the girls.

"Cawvey's gone."

Oh my God! Cawvey! Jessica Cawvey! She is the soldier KIA. The deepest pain I'd ever felt in my life hit me. We all lost it, bawling and hugging. The sadness was unrelenting. *It hurts! It hurts so much! Why God? Why? Why her?*

Trying to see through the darkness of the barracks and through my tears, we grounded their gear in their rooms and retreated to a bunker. A group of our first platoon females sat in the bunker crying together and sharing memories of our amazing friend and battle buddy. As we reminisced, we laughed, but the tears were nonstop. The pain took my breath away and would not allow me to have it back. We all sat in that bunker dreading what we knew was to come—a formation with the entire unit with the absolution of what we didn't want to accept. Why God?

As we chatted through our grief in the bunker, another soldier poked their head in the bunker and said that our unit was being summoned to the MWR building. A feeling all too familiar, and we knew what was about to happen. We tried to hold back the tears and whimpers as we entered the building in the wee hours of the morning. We struggled to not lose it, which was impossible to hold back the pain. The lights were dimmed as we entered the large tin MWR building. Then I saw Willy headed my way. *Oh my God. He doesn't know yet. Oh man.* My heart is about to break some more.

Immediately he saw all of us girls clearly devastated and full of pain. "What? What's going on? What? Tell me! Where's Cawvey?" Willy pleaded for an answer. We struggled to even form the words to speak. We just cried harder, and Andrea dropped to the ground in tears. His face filled with pain and the sadness unleashed. The loss of our Number Two crippled us all.

First Sergeant Lauher entered, and we all just knew what was coming as his gaze pressed the ground during his approach to an open area to address all of us. My muscles tightened, and I was already feeling the devastation of what was about to happen. The somber room was one I couldn't explain.

As he struggled to begin his report, he lost his words. When he was forced to speak Jessica Cawvey's name and report her KIA, he choked up with agony in front of us all.

There was something about seeing a grown man cry that cut deep and pulled at the emotional heart strings. This was far different though. This was *Top!* The One SG, a nickname Cawvster gave him. This was our badass leader in this horrible combat zone.

Stunned, we all stared in horror without words, only whimpers and wails of heartbreak and sadness ... more pain. Some soldiers crumbled to the ground to brace themselves. A picture ... a sound ... a moment ... that forever burned deep.

We all took it hard. Depression set in and some of us couldn't even get out of bed the following few days. I recall one day someone came through our barracks and commented that we needed to get up. I don't even remember who it was. I do remember the female from another platoon came out of her cubicle and snapped, "You leave those girls alone. Let them grieve. They need this time. They will be fine. Just leave them alone."

As the next few days passed, a bunch of first platoon females worked together with one of our sergeants—he was our awesome historian—to make a slideshow for Cawvey's memorial. After the last memorial, a month prior, she made it very clear, "Don't you play that depressing-ass song if I die." She was referring to the same song that was played at each of our fallen four memorials. Although it was a good song, "American Soldier" by Toby Keith was not as comforting after the fourth time. "You better play something like 'Damn It Feels Good to Be a Gangsta' if I die. I also want you to throw my boots over the power lines!" She had said with a laugh and in complete seriousness.

Her memorial was the hardest one I had to go through. She and I shared memories prior to Iraq. Now Hobbs wasn't returning to the base, and Cawvey would never come back.

Dear Lord, make it stop.

An excerpt from Specialist Robert (Willy) Williams's speech at Jessica Cawvey's memorial.

"Me, *Cawvster, and Andrea were known to each other as the Tripod. A tripod doesn't stand without all three legs supporting it. When we thought of it, it was funny, it was a joke. We did so much together, and we were very close. None of us imagined how iconic the term would be if we ever lost a leg of the Tripod. Part of us coping with the reality of this whole morbid affair that we were thrown into was joking around about it. After Morrison and Lamb's ceremony we discussed what song we would want to play at our ceremony. Ridiculous suggestions ranged from "Roll Out" to the theme song from "Charles in Charge". It was our twisted sense of humor. It couldn't and would never happen to us. We discussed that we would want everyone at our ceremonies to know that we cared nothing about the Global War on Terrorism or any of that. If it was our choice, we would not be here. As one of the two remaining members of the Tripod, I hold a great responsibility to say what will surely leave the higher-ranking people at this ceremony shocked. I don't want to do all that because I want people to remember what I had to say about Cawvster and not leave them angry. So just know that what I'm saying is sugarcoated only to the point where Cawvster would be pleased at my final words of her.*

One of the things that was so pleasant about Cawvster was her apathy. This may not seem like a compliment, but she would take it as one. She cared about the important things: her daughter, friends, and family. Every petty thing that people allow to consume their lives was no bother to her. Her lone priority was the people she loved, and when you boil down all the unimportant things, that's really what you're always left with anyway. This made her a very pleasant and thoughtful person."

AN EXCERPT from Specialist Andrea Bryan's speech at The Cawvster's memorial.

"THE PART of Cawvey that touched me the most was how much she cared for me and how she would do everything in her power to protect me, no matter how crazy I thought she was. That night was my first mission, and I was so scared I didn't know what to do. She made sure she was able to go to make sure that her "Number One" wouldn't be scared. Before we got in our trucks to leave, I told her that I was terrified and didn't know if I could do it. Of course, to make me feel better, she told me everything was going to be fine and not to be scared. And instantly, I wasn't."

CAWVEY'S MEMORIAL was the hardest one I had attended. Hearing Andrea and Willy speak about our Cawster silenced the somber room. I remember as Andrea was heading back to her seat, she tripped over one of the wires and let out a quiet, yet obvious, "Shit." It felt as though Cawvster's humor broke the melancholy and a few faces cracked a smile. She was always so good at that. It was second nature to her.

After packing up her things, the barracks felt empty. A huge part of many of us was missing. We were missing Cawvey. Each time I passed by her room, I would glance into her bunk, expecting to see her. It was hard to accept that she would never be there again. The cross necklace that hung from the top bunk, just above where she would lay her head on the bottom bunk, remained.

I made the decision to move from my cubicle with Marisa into Andrea's room. It wasn't an easy one. I had spent the entire deployment as Marisa's bunkmate. She was my solid that I needed. She was my person.

It's rather strange how we all processed our grief differently. For me, I moved into Cawvey's bunk. I wanted to be there for Andrea and to help her feel less alone. Having another body in the room hopefully helped lessen the loss we felt at times. It remained "Cawvey's bunk," but I was just living in it, and we all felt that way.

Unfortunately, I wouldn't understand for years what that did to Marisa. She experienced the loss of Cawvey with us all, then the loss of her roommate who moved a few cubicles down. Years down the road when she told me about the pain and confusion it caused her, my heart broke. I had no idea. Hearing that pain in her voice was something I wanted to take away from her, but I couldn't. I hugged her and pleaded with apologies. "I never meant to hurt you, friend. I was just trying to be there for Andrea," I cried.

The truth is, I didn't just do it for Andrea. I did it for my own selfish reasons. I wanted Cawvey back. I wanted to be as close to her as I could. From that point on, I fell asleep with that cross necklace of hers hanging above my head at night.

"A THOUSAND WORDS won't bring you back, I know because I tried. Neither would a thousand tears, I know because I cried."
Author unknown.

9

THE BLAST THAT CAN KISS MY ASS

HOBBS:

IT WASN'T a typical night mission. Things were different. I wasn't traveling with my normal team, the team I'd rolled out with for nine months. The convoy manifest had changed and was completely different. I was in the rear truck as usual, but this time my platoon sergeant was my driver, and Cawvey was my A-driver. An A-driver is the passenger who is posted up scanning the perimeter with her weapon at the ready.

We loaded up our trucks, and I mounted my 50-cal weapon to the bed of the truck. We hadn't been on the road very long, maybe twenty minutes from the time we left the Baghdad International Airport with our convoy of civilian mail carriers. We had grown quite a bond with this crew. We worked together to get the job done and protected one another. We were just outside of the Abu Ghraib prison when suddenly a light flashed so hot and so strong it shook my soul. That's the last thing I remember before my life changed completely.

The fierce heat of an unexpected roadside bomb enveloped me. I thought my insides got sucked out from the furious blast. A piercing scream came from the near distance. I don't think it came from me, but I'm not completely sure. All I saw was darkness, but I felt pressure so strong on my face. I couldn't even comprehend what had happened. I tried to move my tongue around in my mouth, and immediately I realized it was bad. It was really bad. I felt teeth that had been knocked out moving around in my mouth.

I lay there awake for most of it, but I was in and out at times. I heard some familiar voices talking to me. I responded to them, but I'm not sure they could understand me. I heard them struggling to figure out how to get me out. Then I heard them mention possibly pulling the truck. Holy shit! I was trapped under the five-ton truck!

Struggling to force my busted-out teeth away from the rear of my throat, I saw my driver, Sergeant Edwards, walking around aimlessly. He seemed confused. *Where's Cawvey? I don't hear her voice.*

Then I heard some not-so-familiar voices. A Marine unit stopped by to check on us. Then they were gone. I could hear my unit working together to discuss how to hook up the truck and shift it off my face.

"No, no, no! Bad idea!" I managed to get out through my mouth full of busted teeth and a truck on my face. They heard me and decided to get a jack and jack up the truck. After they jacked up the truck, they got me out. They put me on a stretcher and loaded me onto the medevac helicopter. I was in and out of consciousness, so I woke up sporadically. I didn't see any familiar faces in my haziness, but I felt comfort. I felt as though someone I knew was with me. I felt calmed.

Looking back on it, I may have had that feeling since Sergeant Edwards, my platoon sergeant and driver, was on the same helicopter. Maybe his presence made me feel calmed. Maybe it was the presence of someone that wasn't even there, like God or a guardian angel.

As the helicopter team lowered me on a stretcher from the helicopter, one of the four corners gave out and hit the ground on my descent. Thank God it wasn't far because even that small bounce off the ground sent more pain through my body. I saw soldiers running all around me securing supplies and hooking me up as they rolled my stretcher to a nearby building. I heard the propellers on the helicopter speed up as it took off back into the Iraqi sky. I heard one of them say, "He's waking up." I realized they were cutting my pants off. *Oh shit, my balls are about to be out.* Then all went dark again.

At the shittiest time possible, I woke up and felt as though I was suffocating. *I can't breathe! Holy shit, I'm going to die!* I realized they were putting in a breathing tube and in the midst of my panic, I passed out again.

When I finally woke up, I was lying in a hospital bed in the Baghdad Hospital. I turned my head to get a look at the guy next to me. *Oh, well hell, why'd I look?* The guy next to me was all burnt up from head to toe. He appeared to be an Iraqi boy.

Ain't this a bitch! One minute I was back from leave doing my typical daily job, then *boom.* Literally a *boom,* and I would never be as I was. As I lay there helpless, I got the urgency to pee. I frantically buzzed for the nurse, and she finally entered after what seemed like three minutes. I told her I had to go to the bathroom so bad and pee, and I was adamant. With a reassuring tone, she responded, "You have a catheter in. You don't have to go to the bathroom, just go when you need to."

Confused, I didn't argue and just trusted her. Then I was out again. I thought I was dreaming when I heard some familiar voices. Struggling to open my eyes because they were swollen shut, I could see people. Struggling to see past the tubes, I saw

Jen standing next to my hospital bed. Marisa, Joy, and a few others were there as well.

"Hey, I love you! I miss you," Jen told me.

"I love you," I managed to get out. "Do I have any hot nurses?" I asked with an attempt at a smile.

Laughing, Jen said, "Oh, you are going to be just fine."

"Is Cawvey okay?" I asked them. I assumed Sergeant Edwards was okay since I had seen him. I never saw her.

They all looked around at one another, and I knew instantly what they were going to say. "She didn't make it. She died instantly from the blast."

What? The pain, deep, direct, and worse than the stupid-ass tubes and broken face. Cawvey was a mom! She was a young, single mom. *It should've been me! God damn it! It should have been me!*

I wasn't at the Baghdad hospital too long before they flew me to Germany. I remember waking up on the C-130, flying. I saw stacks and stacks of stretchers with casualties. They definitely weren't stingy with the pain meds on that flight. They kept us knocked out which was quite a relief.

After a few weeks in Germany, they flew me to Walter Reed Hospital in Bethesda, Maryland. Talk about a shitty place to be. I felt super distraught as I was surrounded by a bunch of soldiers in much worse shape than I was, or at least I thought so. I didn't belong there. These guys needed way more attention than I did. The army came to their senses and realized that Walter Reed wasn't the place for me. They shipped me off to Fort Knox, Kentucky, to continue my recovery.

Fort Knox had never had someone like me: missing my upper jaw with crushed bone fragments all the way up past the nasal cavity near my skull and brain. You could tell they had absolutely no idea what to do with me. Apparently, it was a learning experience for them. Awesome! I'm all about learning experiences, but this time I was the test dummy for these *oh-so-qualified* Army doctors.

Bitterness came with time. I don't want to seem as though I doubted the abilities of the doctors, but ... that's exactly what I'm saying. They had no idea how to handle me and my injuries. They posted me up in a hospital on base and strung me around on a daily basis. Some days I had five or six appointments, and other days I had none. I had nothing to do and no purpose. I had nothing positive to thrive on or to find a bit of satisfaction in.

Fort Knox wired my mouth shut after they tried to take out everything that was shattered. Initially all they did was remove all the bone fragments. Then they tried to pull my palate down —what palate I had left. The pain was relentless, and I had never experienced anything like that including having a five-ton truck on my face.

I woke up just as they finished the implantation of the wires in my mouth. The doctor told me, "Yeah, we are going to see what happens." I didn't really get a vibe of confidence. *They have no idea if this is going to work! Good God!*

A few more weeks pass by, and suddenly, Thanksgiving Day is approaching. I was desperate to eat. I tried to convince the doctor at Fort Knox to cut my wires the day before Thanksgiving. I was persuasive. He was hesitant at first but said, "Well, I guess we could just cut them and then you can come back after Thanksgiving to have them removed."

"Yes, take these fuckers out," I pushed through my wires.

The doc cut my wires. He literally just snipped them and did nothing else with them so I could eat some food for Thanksgiving. I was not going to back down from the ever-so-tempting idea of eating real food. I hadn't tasted real food in almost two months. I was so excited to eat something other than a liquid diet.

Unfortunately, that turned out not to be the best idea. It wasn't at all the exhilarating experience I had anticipated. Instead, it was uncomfortable and painful as the wires hit both the top and bottom of my mouth as I attempted to chew.

After Thanksgiving I headed back to Fort Knox. They took my wires out, and I continued with tons of appointments. Some of the leaders in charge tried to make me follow their rules and expectations, but clearly, they didn't know me. I continued doing my own thing, and I didn't follow their expectations. I mean, seriously? They wanted me to climb out of my bed, missing all my teeth, only to report to some bullshit formation in the morning for accountability. No one here gave a shit about me or where I was at.

Things got a little better when I became aware of two other 1544th members who were also at Fort Knox on med hold. So, I hunted them down at some barracks located on the base. Whenever I got the chance, I ventured out of the hospital on my own and went to visit them. We rendezvoused together and then I returned to my prison, the room I had at the hospital.

One day I went to the barracks to visit them, and I was approached by one of the leaders on duty. He asked me my name and glanced at his clipboard thinking that I was an incoming soldier needing to be processed into their barracks.

I wasn't sure if this guy was going to be pissed that I was over hanging out at the barracks I didn't live at. So, I went with the flow and told him my name.

"Ryan Hobbs? Yep, we got you down on the list. Go ahead and get your mattress and bedding, and you'll be right in here."

You can only imagine what I did. Duh, I grabbed my bedding and reported to my bunk like a good little soldier.

This was madness and completely messed up! Knox had me down in two different places. I had a room at the hospital and a room at the barracks. These guys couldn't even keep tabs on me. This allowed me to go visit my battle buddies, and when they had to wake up and go to formation, I just stayed in bed. At both the barracks and in the hospital, everyone was expected to have duties. Typical duties like cleaning and barracks maintenance. As for me, I had none. I am pretty good at what I do—blow off things I don't want to deal with. That's how I roll.

10

MY BROWN ENVELOPE ARRIVES

JEN:

"BUFF, YOU GOT LEAVE." The words were so unexpected and left me questioning what I'd just heard. *Is this a dream?* Home seemed like a distant memory. One of my leaders handed me the infamous brown envelope I thought I'd never see. The dates October 30 to November 14 were written on it in black permanent marker. My heart raced, and I could hear myself breathing as if I'd just run a few miles. Without tearing it open like a child at Christmastime, I tried to be cool and calm when I opened it. I pulled out the papers with my orders to ship me home on a two-week leave. *Momma, I'm coming home!*

I hustled to the MWR and jumped on the phone to call my brother, Scott, and tell him about my upcoming leave. We planned to keep it a secret from my mom, and we formed a plan to surprise her. Scott filled my stepdad in on it, and he helped us carry out my surprise arrival.

October 30th finally arrived, and I boarded a plane to

return home. Stepping off the plane in Illinois, the sun shone brightly on the beautiful afternoon. I'd never been so happy to feel the chilly weather in the Midwest.

Another first platoon battle buddy of mine, Reno, was on his leave at the same time. What a relief it was to venture home into the unknown with another battle buddy because I certainly didn't want to do it alone. As we walked down the ramp exiting nearby the security checkpoint, I saw Hobbs waiting for me. I was used to seeing him in his BDUs or his physical training getup; it was so different to see him dressed in jeans and a sweater, looking so handsome.

Finally, the embrace I had been waiting for. I hadn't seen him since my brief visit to the Baghdad hospital the morning after his accident. Seeing him now brought a feeling of safety and comfort which covered me like a weighted blanket.

Reno's family also came to the airport. They were beyond elated to see him, and I watched as they showered him with love and kisses. It was a day to cherish forever.

Hobbs and I got to spend a few hours together. We had dinner and couldn't stop talking. As the sun started to set that evening, I noticed the sky looked far different than what I was used to in the past year.

As the sun disappeared on the horizon, everything else that was so far different than what I was used to, became very transparent. There were lights, cars, people, and action. It was strange to respond to a different kind of "action," whereas my past year was spent responding to "combat action".

My time with Hobbs that evening came to an end. My brother, Scott, picked me up so we could return to my hometown and carry out our exciting plan. We pulled quietly into the driveway of my parents' house. It was dark, but I could see the adorable ranch they had purchased while I was gone. A quaint, white one-story with shutters welcomed me home in the dark silence as my brother and I crept up to the door. He had already called and communicated with my stepdad that we were near arrival. We rang the doorbell, and I waited anxiously. On the other side of the door, I heard Mike playing his part with confusion and wonder.

"Who is at the door this time of night?" I was so excited to hear his voice and hug him! I could hardly contain myself.

He opened the door, and I quickly wrapped myself into him for a big quiet hug. Then I made my way down the unknown hallway of my parents' new home. Toward the faint light coming from the room at the end of the hall, I turned and crossed the threshold of the door into my parents' bedroom. It was then that I saw my beautiful mother lying in bed watching TV. I ran to her and covered her with my embrace with plans to never let go.

I was back in my mother's arms, and tears of happiness overcame us. She could barely speak through her shock and tears. Finally, I had the safety and comfort I'd been yearning for from the most important person in my life. *This is the best feeling in the world!* I couldn't even begin to imagine what this must feel like as a mother. Her child—the same child she'd worried about every day over the last nine months—safely back in her arms.

For a moment, my mind wasn't stuck in Iraq. The moment was brief and quickly passed. I found myself trying to remember how to act in this civilian life. Emotions felt so foreign, and I found myself just going through the motions because I hadn't lived them in so long. It was rather unfamiliar now. I tried to understand the feelings I was having, being away from my unit and the family I had endured so much with in the past ten months.

Ten months seemed like a lifetime, and that foreign life I had been living didn't fit in well as a civilian. The term *citi-*

zen/soldier took on a whole new meaning for me. I found myself struggling to be present in conversations and sometimes faking it.

The fleeting few weeks that followed were full of good times and bewilderment. Time with friends, a party in my honor, a visit from my other brother, Jake, whom I hadn't seen in years. Then another surprise as we picked up my granny from the train station. I recall her letting out a few cuss words of shock. She was so thrilled and, of course, cried along with me as we hugged outside the train station.

Hobbs visited me in Lincoln, and for the first time ever, we were finally a couple outside of the Army and combat zone. I was shocked that Fort Knox let him get away to come see me. Then in classy Hobbs fashion, he filled me in on the secret that he wasn't given permission to come. He just left.

Trying to forget that he was technically on AWOL status, we attempted to enjoy the days together without allowing the expected, inevitable end to approach. In a conversation one night, he shared some memories from October 6th with me that were too fresh for him to talk about yet, so we somewhat steered away from those deep conversations. We knew there would come a time in which we would have to face the trauma, yet neither of us were ready for that.

The end of my leave came faster than I had hoped, but there was no getting around it. It was time to return to the 1544th, and Hobbs would have to stay behind, going through what would be two years of med-hold madness with the Department of Veterans Affairs (VA). It was the worst experience of his life, which was a baffling statement when you were talking about a pillar of strength who withstood and survived a *five-ton* truck on his face.

I returned to the airport. Another perplexing experience with more feelings of excitement, sadness, and overwhelming disorientation. Going back to the combat zone was far different than heading over the first time. The first time, I had no idea what to expect. On my return home, I knew what was to come because I'd been there. Ten months down, unsure of how many more to go ... without Hobbs.

"See you soon, family," I tried to stifle tears so hot they stung even my heart.

11

A COIN THAT MEANT THE WORLD

JEN:

THE MONTHS that followed the explosion are hard to remember and accept. My actions aren't something I am proud of, but I do believe that I shouldn't beat myself up over it. I have learned to grant myself some grace. We all deal with trauma differently and grieve differently. We all experience our own war, even after our return.

As for me, I was a lost young lady in a combat zone. Lost from reality, lost from security that was no longer there. Hobbs's and my conversations on the phone were rare and hard for both of us. He struggled, as did I. Our struggles were significantly different, yet with similar emotions. I had absolutely no clue what he was going through, whereas he was no longer able to relate to my situation since he was in a whirlwind of madness himself.

As I continued on our deployment, he was in limbo at Walter Reed Hospital and Fort Knox. The harsh and bitter truth was that I had lost touch of myself. I felt like Hobbs and I started to grow apart. The conversations were depressing on the phone. He barely even talked to me. The days continued to be hard and trying.

Still doing our normal mail routes, we also took on morgue runs. It wasn't a long convoy; you just had to transport bodies from one place to another at the nearby base connected to the Baghdad International Airport. Those missions were not required and went on a volunteer basis. One day, I volunteered to do the morgue run. I'm not sure what the hell I was thinking. Our unit had been through so much in the last few months that I was growing numb and detached from reality.

The first part of the mission was to drive to the hospital at the Green Zone and secure the deceased before taking them to the morgue. They would remain there until they were flown home. So, I arrived at the hospital, dismounted from my truck, and waited as they loaded up the two stretchers with the black body bags into the bed of my truck. Two United States soldiers were loaded up, and two plastic ziplock baggies were handed to me. *Um, what the hell is this? I did not sign up for this.*

"These are the items that were gathered from the deceased. They will travel with you, and you are to make sure they stay with the bodies at the morgue," a man in scrubs told me.

In complete shock, I secured them in my hands. "Roger that," I replied and climbed into the driver's seat of my truck. I placed the bags next to me and tried not to look at them. It felt strange not to have an A-driver with me. I was alone in the cab of this truck, waiting for the convoy to roll out so we could deliver the deceased to the morgue. *The deceased.* Those words played over and over in my head. It felt so sad. They have names. They have families.

Don't do it, Jennifer. I looked down at the baggies. I saw their IDs. I then knew the names of the deceased soldiers in my truck. In one of the bags, just under the dog tags, I saw a photo —his family. My heart became heavy, and I started to pray.

Dear Lord, be with these soldiers as they travel safely back home where they will be laid to rest. Be with their family and friends through their times of heartbreak and struggle. This I ask in Jesus' name, Amen.

I'd never been in a morgue. It looked nothing like I imagined it would. There were large cooler-looking buildings sitting on the Iraqi sand. It was hard to hand over the ziplock bags. I didn't even know the soldiers, but it was difficult to let them go. I stood in awe as the stretchers were unloaded and relocated into the cooler. Just like that, the mission was completed. We loaded up and headed back to Mortaritaville.

Shortly after, in December, a position on force protection opened up. Force protection was made up of various duties split among soldiers from all the units on our base. I volunteered for the position, which was to staff the Northgate, one of the two entrances to our base. I thought if I could get off the road then it might help the tragedy pass faster, or at least I hoped so. It seemed like the best thing to do.

The gate of our base was only about fifteen hundred meters from Abu Ghraib. Since most military vehicles used the safer gate on the south side of our base, our job was to be a lookout. From time to time, people approached our base, and we would have to check their IDs before allowing them to enter. Some civilians entered our base for various jobs. Those were the times we had to do searches while other soldiers stood guard. It wasn't a busy gate, but there were a few occasions when devastating things occurred.

One day after a huge roadside bomb went off only one thousand meters away, a unit that was on patrol brought the civilian casualty in through the Northgate. The looks on their faces was something I will never forget. The soldiers dismounted their tanks in armored vehicles and gathered around the back of one of their Humvees. They all took a corner of a tarp and carried it with their heads hung in despair. The tarp sagged in just one spot with the remains of the deceased. There wasn't much left. Those are the images that are impossible to erase from your memory.

The early mornings were glorious sitting on the berm at Northgate watching the sunrise and listening to the birds sing. Looking into the beautiful sky took me to another place. But as soon as I brought my gaze down, the early morning light shone upon Abu Ghraib and all the sand surrounding the walls of our base. I was brought back to reality. But the sky and sunrise gave me a quick taste of the reality I remembered. Just for a moment, the war zone disappeared, and I inhaled the crisp morning air as I remembered calmer mornings of coffee and conversations with my college roommate.

I staffed the Northgate with two other soldiers from different units. We spent most of our time playing cards, telling stories, watching movies on a laptop, and responding to radio calls whenever the watchtowers called in movement. Two cooked meals a day were delivered on a Humvee. Bathroom breaks were nearby in the sweltering hot Porta-Potty. This was nothing new, but sometimes we had the luxury of trailers with toilets. Cooked meals and a Porta-Potty were also luxuries.

During this time, I tried to cope with everything, including Hobbs being gone. I struggled with our loss of Cawvey and wondered how her family and daughter were doing. Hobbs also struggled. He had been in constant chaos throughout his recovery since his transition back home. Things were definitely not easy for him or any wounded soldier. I can't even imagine.

As I continued taking on each moment at a time, I felt adrift in my detached existence from what used to be my real life. My relationship with Hobbs crumbled as I tried to explain how I felt alone and how I needed him. I felt like he wasn't there for me. He was always so negative on the phone which had quite an effect on my mindset. I needed him there ... there in the moment ... even if he wasn't there in the combat zone. I needed him to be there with me and for me. I heard the hurt, anger, and confusion in his voice.

Good grief, it sounded so selfish, but that was the reality of my lame choices. Excuse me while I hang my head. I was putting a band-aid on a gaping wound. How could I do this to him? What the hell was my problem? I kicked him when he was at his lowest. The break-up phone call was excruciating, but the feelings that followed are ridiculously hard to explain.

I was trying to survive. I couldn't understand the last few months and was angry at the cards I was dealt.

What a stinking pity party, right? Yeah, tell me about it. These are the decisions I have dealt with in my life.

My choices quickly caught up to me as I got my ass handed to me shortly after. Standing at a position all too familiar, parade rest, I found myself in front of the new battalion officers that I didn't even know. Since we were close to rolling out of country and the new rotations were starting, new units were coming in as we prepared for our departure. The battalion in charge was being replaced by another unit that had just arrived in country, so they got stuck handing me my lame-ass Article 15, a discipline practice in which you are often demoted. I was only a few months away from my opportunity toward the next rank of E-5 Sergeant, and I got my E-4 Specialist rank taken from me. I was demoted to E-3 Private First Class for admitting to drinking when questioned, but never caught.

A FEW DAYS PRIOR:

. . .

Blue Falcon—the term we use in the military to describe when someone screws others for their own good. This was my situation when Lieutenant Blue Falcon overheard a conversation in the girls' barracks from a nearby cubicle. She must have heard some of us talking about how we got to hang around a campfire the night before and enjoy some wine. Her cubicle was next to many other females, but she didn't know exactly who it was that had said it.

After a platoon meeting, she pulled aside all of us females who lived within a certain vicinity from her cubicle. Without telling our squad leaders, platoon sergeant, or any other high-ranking official in our unit, she confronted us females. "Were you all in your bunks at curfew last night?" she questioned accusingly. Wide-eyed, we all nodded.

"Well, I hope you are telling me the truth because there is an investigation going on with the Bravo Company, and if any of you were there last night ..." she continued, but I didn't hear the words as my mind started to wander.

Oh crap, here it comes. My honesty and integrity are about to get the best of me.

"Well, I was over there, but I was in my bunk at curfew like I was supposed to be," I told her and didn't bust anyone else out that was with me.

"Were you drinking?" She looked at me with a pissed off expression which was rather confusing since she was no angel herself.

"Yes." I admitted.

The Blue Falcon flew straight to the new battalion and jumped past all higher ranks in our unit to report me. Awesome!

My decision to drink wine that evening was my choice. It may be considered a bad choice to some, but there were much worse things going on by the actions of others. Alcohol wasn't a common thing for us since we didn't exactly have easy access to it. There were some people who managed to mail it to you, but that was not a common thing, and it definitely didn't happen to everyone. Another unit on our base stumbled upon a large CONEX full of wine. Since my twenty-first birthday was in the next couple of days, it was exciting to have the opportunity to have a glass of wine to celebrate it.

A few days later, on my twenty-first birthday, I was waiting for my leadership so we could head over to battalion for my Article 15 ass-handing meeting. I had seen the first sergeant earlier, and he told me, "Sorry Buff, you know if I would've caught you, you'd just be sweeping the sidewalks." I believed him because I wasn't the first. Others were actually caught. Like I said, worse things had happened. I was just the first to admit it when questioned without getting caught.

While we were sitting on the bench waiting for the first sergeant, Lieutenant Blue Falcon strolled up. She swooped in and sat next to me on the bench. "Don't let this get you down, Buff. We all make mistakes. It'll be fine and then you can move on," she stated. I couldn't believe she had the audacity to say that to me after being the one who reported my admission statement. I didn't respond.

Standing at parade rest in front of the new battalion commander, my leaders were given the opportunity to speak on my behalf. They spoke words of encouragement and strength; they discussed my work ethic and the true soldier that I am. When they got around the table to Lieutenant Blue Falcon, she started talking about how much of a great soldier I was. She reiterated everything all my leaders had just said about me. *Are you kidding me right now?*

I didn't know what she was trying to gain from it. Regardless, I was demoted to private first class and dismissed from parade rest. I exited the room, and the new command sergeant major told me to come into her office.

Damn it! Hasn't this torture been enough? What else do I have to endure?

She shut the door, and I snapped to parade rest.

"At ease soldier, take a seat," she ordered. "Your leadership thinks very highly of you. You are an asset to the military. The Army needs women like you. Don't let this get you down. Learn from it and move on. You understand soldier?"

"Yes, Sergeant Major," I said with pride.

After our conversation I stood up to leave, and she shook my hand. As our hands connected, I felt the coin she passed into the palm of my hand. Handing others a coin is a tradition in the military that gets rather old after random people give you coins just because they visit and speak a few words of encouragement to the masses. This coin was extraordinary for me, and the conversation will live with me forever. Her words lifted me up just when I needed it most. It is a conversation I will never forget.

12

THE WELCOMING OF A LIFETIME

Jen:

We finally received a tentative date to leave Iraq and head to Kuwait. We convoyed in two different fleets. I was on the second one of course, considering I hadn't earned any special privilege to flee early having been demoted just weeks before our departure.

We left some of our up-armored vehicles behind for another unit, but most of them would return to the United States by barge. Before they did however, we were expected to clean every last grain of sand out of the sneaky cracks and crevices. I somehow got lucky and was never put on this detail.

Once they were all cleaned and ready to take to port, we convoyed together, one last time. I rode in a truck with Marisa. It was just the two of us, and it felt so weird after a year of riding in groups of three or four, loaded with ammo, and always on edge so as not to become complacent. Kuwait was so different though. It was almost like you could relax a bit, even though it was hard, and part of you was always scanning and very aware of your surroundings.

"Dude, I have to pee," I said with panic in my voice to Marisa.

"Are you serious right now?" she laughed. "Well, you better pee in a bottle."

"Oh my gosh, I suck at that," I laughed nervously. I had no choice but to grab the water bottle and attempt the impossible for the second time this deployment. Well, apparently it is not impossible. It might have helped if I'd have cut off the top of the water bottle. Complete fail, again!

"Crap! It's going all over," I said, but I couldn't help but laugh.

"Oh, my God, it smells. Dude you are going to get us into so much trouble," Marisa responded, still cracking up.

It was leaking out of the hole in the floorboards, and that gave me an idea. I grabbed a bottle of water and tried to rinse the floorboard out more and force it toward the drain hole.

"Oh my gosh, I hope no one finds out. They are going to be so pissed." Marisa pointed out the obvious piss pun, and we laughed uncontrollably.

We pulled into port, and our ground guides motioned us where to park. Marisa and I hopped out immediately, securing all our belongings and snapped, "Alright, we're all good here! Let's roll out." No one checked our truck, and we all loaded up onto buses without even looking back. I was so relieved.

"Holy cow, that was close," I whispered to Marisa as we were still laughing.

We return to the USA, hip hip hooray. Finally, safe solid ground ... or was it? We didn't know what was in store for us. The hardest days were yet to come for some of us, maybe most of us, possibly all.

We arrived at Fort McCoy, Wisconsin. As our plane

slowed down on the tarmac, I saw in the distance out my window a crowd standing near the hanger. People were jumping up and down and waving signs, and they were not wearing military uniforms.

We dismounted and saw crowds of families waiting anxiously to smother us with their love. Although the cold pierced my skin, the tears of relief and happiness flowed out of my eyes, warming my skin. I couldn't walk fast enough to get to the crowd. Pure joy radiated off all our faces.

We finally got closer to the families, and I scanned their faces to find my family. It was so cold, and everyone was bundled up in coats and winter weather gear, so it was hard to see people.

I found them!

I rushed over to my mom and stepdad, dropped my bags, and found the perfect place to fold myself right up into their hugs. That was one day I will never forget.

We got to spend some time with our families, but it was short-lived. They had to head back home while we went through a few days of out-processing. Back at the barracks, we grounded our gear and waited for orders. There we were, back in Fort McCoy again, in the freezing dead of winter.

Oh snap, look who came to be with us at Fort McCoy! It's Hobbs.

Oh shit! I had to face my demons earlier than expected. I bet he hated me. I needed to talk to him. Time to own my actions and figure this out.

Hobbs's radiant smile was still gleaming even with the missing teeth. He scooped my heart up right where it was left. Not fair for him, but certainly not fair for either of us. Struggle was ahead of us, but the love was still so strong. Together and apart, we had already endured so much in such a short time.

Hobbs was rocking a bright red shirt that read, "I work at

my McJob." Everyone was so happy to see him. His seemingly effortless positivity and uplifting spirit gave us all hope. He is certainly a gift. He finds humor in anything. This annoys me at times, but usually it's a breath of fresh air.

We were at Fort McCoy for about a week and had to sit through so many briefings. Who in the world was even listening to any of it? It may have been valuable information, but all I could think about was how close we were to home. I was sure I wasn't the only one. And if they weren't thinking about home, they were probably recalling memories of the last fifteen months. The anticipation of home was not all exciting. It was also such a scary feeling. It was intimidating. An outpouring of information during out-processing was not easy to inhale when you were still in shock. Yikes! What a mess! The adrenaline, confusion, and anticipation of being home and expecting the unexpected was not the time to trust our attention to detail. That immediate overload of briefings during out-processing, I think, is something that can certainly be improved to help a soldier's transition back.

We finally got to leave Fort McCoy, and we were lucky to be on charter buses. We were headed back to Paris, Illinois. The last time we were on that route, we were leaving our home behind, just starting our deployment. This time was different as some of us were watching movies on the bus TVs, whereas others were taking a nap or listening to music with their headphones plugged in. Other people were on their phones texting their loved ones since they'd secured their phones at Fort McCoy during the family visits. The scene around me was far different than what that ride looked like fifteen months ago.

As we crossed the state border into Illinois from Wisconsin, a police escort picked us up. We were escorted by the police the rest of the way back, and just as we were about an hour from Paris, we all quickly became aware of the hovering helicopter following our convoy. For returning soldiers from a combat zone, that wasn't something that would go unnoticed. As we all looked out the windows to assess the situation, we realized it was a news helicopter, and it followed our buses.

Each overpass we came to, fire trucks and other first responders waved and hung American flags. When we were ten miles out from Paris, the streets started to fill up with people scattered along the sides. I couldn't even believe it. For the last ten miles of our trip, we gazed in complete awe. The community of Paris extended for miles.

This is for us?

Roads were shut down, and students were let out from school. The welcome home ceremony was by far one of the best days to remember from our 1544th history. Words can't describe the overwhelming emotions I felt in that homecoming. After a year of being withdrawn from our lives, our family, and our world as we knew it, suddenly we were being celebrated all around us. Humbling to say the least. Some handled it with grace, others with uncertainty, and others with complete dismay.

After a fifteen-month deployment with much heartache and trauma, I don't think any of us expected a welcoming like this. I'm not sure why we didn't expect anything. I guess the detachment from home makes you feel like you've been forgotten. Some of your family misses you and maybe some of your friends, but you have no idea that an entire community has missed you and has eagerly been waiting for your return.

Andrea, Jen & Willy back in America at last

Jen & Hobbs at Fort McCoy before Iraq

Jen & Hobbs during Jen's leave from Iraq

Jen & Marisa

Jen as the driver

Candyland in Iraq with Bert, Joy & Jen

Cawvster and Jen in Balad, Iraq

Hobbs and Shaun in Fort McCoy

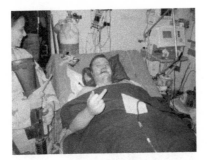

Hobbs's response to the roadside bomb

Hobbs...always breaking the rules

Jojo, Serena, Jen & Andrea at *The Faces of the Fallen* exhibit in Washington, D.C

My family when I was on leave from Iraq. Me, mom, stepdad & my brother Scott

My favorite picture of the Cawvster

Nick, Hobbs & Joy

Nick, Hobbs & Shaun

Number One and Number Two

Oct. 6th prior to mission- Cawvster, SGT.
Edwards, Andrea & Marisa, Jen in front.

Reno, Hobbs, and Jen

The Tripod

13

R & R: MISSING-IN-ACTION STYLE

Hobbs:

I was completely tired of being strung around and forgotten —well, forgotten until some egotistical asshole wants to feel better about himself. Finally, my inpatient status switched to a different med hold status. They were going to allow me to go back home where I would continue med hold status and report to my unit daily. *Is this a joke? I have no teeth, I do nothing but wait to hear about the next appointment, and you want me to drive an hour to my unit to sit there and do nothing?* Even my leadership found it asinine and agreed to let me call and check in daily instead of making the long haul there for no reason.

Typically, a med hold soldier was expected to remain at a post and wait to receive treatment at that post. Things looked different for me since I was in the National Guard. The VA fee-based me out to another hospital because the extensive work I needed could not be done at the VA.

Although I was in the comfort of my home, the depression

set in. As I wallowed in my sorrows of captivity, I heard that the 1544th was returning from Iraq. Since the Army expected me to check in with my unit, that was exactly what I decided to do. I drove up to Fort McCoy with Sergeant Edwards, the same guy who was injured in the truck with me. We drove up with another battle buddy and posted up to greet our returning family after the deployment that we didn't get to finish with them.

To say I wished I could've finished the deployment with them is the understatement of a lifetime. I would've done anything not to endure what I'd been going through, followed by what the Army and VA were still putting me through. I wouldn't wish this struggle on anyone.

Finally, that moment, the one I'd waited for, yet not with complete happiness, Jen was there. She was alive and she had returned from Iraq. I was happy to see her even though she broke my heart. The happiness didn't last long as I caught wind of rumors that Jen was seeing some dude from another unit. *Are you freaking kidding me? Of course, she was! Why not kick me when I'm down? Seems everything and everyone else has!*

I didn't take well to the news. Who would? I was pissed off. There I was against military orders, trying to see the girl who broke my heart, and that tramp had been seeing another guy.

She apologized and tried to explain herself. I didn't have many words to offer her and her lame excuses. I just stared at her with some sort of expectation. I didn't know what it was I wanted, but I wanted to show her what she had done to me and make her catch a glimpse of my pain.

Feeling defeated by the previous months, I still couldn't help but feel the same for her. She had my heart, and I never got it back. Honestly, I never wanted it back, even if she did drop me like a bad habit, *after I was blown up!* Who does that?

During my visit, I got called into the First Sergeant

Lauher's office. *Say what? How is this even possible. Haven't I paid my dues? I'm not even here with them. What could I possibly be having to report to his office for?*

"Hobbs, Fort Knox is calling for you. They are asking where you are," he inquired.

Oh, that's why I was called in here.

I had known him for quite some time. Let's recall, this was the same sergeant who witnessed me giving my two weeks after being smoked at drill by the lieutenant. He was used to my shenanigans, yet clearly still frustrated, and I didn't blame him. There he was trying to transition his soldiers back from our fifteen-month deployment, busy I'm sure, and then having to address yet another phone call.

"Well, did you tell them I'm here?" I responded sarcastically, but I was completely serious. Immediately my thoughts wandered. *Of freaking course. They don't care about me and my location until I am finally somewhere I want to be.*

My short visit to Fort McCoy came to an end, and it was time to return to reality, which was starting to seem more like a sick nightmare. I returned to see the unit in Paris at the welcome home ceremony. Some of my family came to attend, which was awesome, but I couldn't even focus and take in the moment. There were people everywhere. It was so loud, and I was surrounded by too much stimulation. I couldn't hear what my family was saying to me. *When is this going to be over?*

Feeling vulnerable in the sea of bodies, I scanned left to right feeling insecure and anxious. When it was finally over, Jen was released from Paris and headed home with her mom and grandma. I went home ... alone ... again.

Jen and I gave another shot at our relationship. I wasn't ready to trust her again, but I wasn't ready to stop loving her or the idea of us either. I was still reporting all over God's green earth for appointments, so I made a beeline off the route to stop and see Jen.

Things seemed to be going well, or at least I thought so. Jen came over often and stayed out at my house. It started to feel like maybe she did like me. Our late-night talks about the explosion ripped open a wound that still hadn't healed. Memories flooded back along with the tears and heartache.

Jen would massage my upper jaw to relieve the tension built up from the bone graft. After my recent bone graft, the doctor suggested this would be one way to relieve that tension and pain. Using bone from my ilium, the back of my hip bone, they rebuilt the upper part of my jawbone. Of course, this came after digging, and I mean *digging* out all the bone fragments that were crushed and scattered into my upper jaw and beyond. The recovery was excruciating.

You would think that getting your face smashed in would be the worst part of all of this. But, if I am being honest, I would say the guilt was far more unbearable. Cawvey ... she was gone. Her daughter, now without her mom. Why? Why not me? I didn't have kids to live for and take care of. I didn't deserve life over her. Why God?

Living a life after such trauma takes a great deal of work. Life shouldn't take work. The only real happiness I got from life at that point was working on my motorcycle or spending time with Jen. Even then though, the pain and guilt haunted us like a dark cloud. It wasn't sustainable. I couldn't live like that. I didn't even feel good about being awake. I wanted to sleep all the time or do something to take my mind off what was real.

Then there was one night when my friend Greg, Jen, and I hit up an old bar I used to work at. I don't remember much, so I'm sure I'd had a bit too much to drink. I woke up at home. I didn't drive luckily, but where was Jen?

After reading the text messages she sent me, I realized she

left me again! Just as I expected. As I read through the text messages, I saw I never texted her back, and clearly, she seemed pissed. I thought we were having a good time. I don't exactly remember it, but I'm a good time! Why wouldn't we have had a good time? I used to go to that particular bar often, so let's just say, I was a preferred customer.

Not sure what all transpired that night. All I know is Jen left and didn't come back.

14

INSTABILITY

JEN:

I'M sure it's clear by now that I was dealing with some issues. I was oblivious to issues Hobbs was dealing with. Why? I'll never know what Hobbs endured and continues to live with. That's not something most people, including myself, can relate to.

For me, after a year or so of instability including a DUI charge (no conviction), motorcycle rides in the sunset with Hobbs, so much love, yet so much pain, Hobbs and I still hadn't dealt with things. There were things that needed to be confronted, conversations that we didn't want to have. Well, yeah, duh ... why would we? Who was making us? Or better yet, who was encouraging us?

For two veterans fresh out of a combat zone with a great deal of trauma on so many different levels, this was where the breakdown came in during the transition process. The actual transition back to civilian life only starts when you return home. Then from there—boom! Sink or float. Dropped into a life you aren't yet transitioned back into, you don't respond well to the situations that seem so new.

So, I split my time between school and my arduous relationship with Hobbs. Our relationship took much work, yet it was so easy to feel.

I was managing a part-time job, a full-time college course load, living in an apartment alone—I felt like I was doing damn well. *Look at me! I can buy my own groceries, my car is paid off, and I'm good.* I was living the dream, right?

Oh, my goodness. Yikes! Sometimes, we find ourselves in these circumstances and are completely naive. Who are you? What are you doing? What exactly do you want?

I reached my breaking point with Hobbs one night when we were at a bar and grill he used to work at. I was sitting at the bar next to his friend, Greg, and Hobbs, who was clearly three sheets to the wind, was at the end of the bar. He was chatting it up with an old female friend. As they got closer to one another, giggling and flirting, I started to get really pissed off. It was clear that this was an old "friend," and she was not being shy. She was all snuggled up to him, whispering in his ear. He was clearly loving every second of it with that shit-eating grin he was wearing. He looked over at me from time to time to acknowledge that I was still there. My glares didn't faze his mood. He was having a great time. His great time came at a cost.

I sat there in awe. My heart was beating out of my chest, and I tried to contain my anger from unleashing. I sipped my beer and felt the heat creep up my neck onto my face.

"I'm going to go to jail if I stay here," I said to Greg.

Greg was easygoing and sensed the severity of the situation.

"Yeah, Ryan's being dumb. I don't know what he's doing," Greg replied.

I made the best choice I could that night. I left. I left without causing a scene or even trying to get the last word in. I drove a few hours home that night. No phone call, no text from Hobbs. Just a quiet ride to myself, dwelling on what had just happened and how easily he allowed it to happen. I didn't even recognize Hobbs that night.

I was done. I was over it. Time to move on. I headed home with no plans of returning. I registered for classes again so I could return to school in the summer and get back to my plan: schooling then a career.

The end of May rolled around, and since I hadn't heard a peep out of the community college I registered with, I followed up to see about my schedule. Turned out the paperwork wasn't completed in time by the processing center, leaving me stuck for the summer. By stuck, I mean stuck in the same circumstances with nothing to do other than to work. Talk about pissing in my Cheerios.

Therefore, I had to revamp my plans yet again. Something I'd become accustomed to. Adapt and overcome, right? That's what they trained us to do in the military. I got a cashier job at a restaurant. I have great people skills, and I am probably one of the most patient people you will ever meet. I am not, however, an asset for restaurant customer service. True statement.

Here's a big shocker. In the midst of my post-traumatic stress, I reunited with an ex. I don't think it needs to be said aloud, but I am a big girl, and I can own it. Relationships are where I have made some of my most shameful decisions. I've hurt so many that I loved and cared about. The truth is hard to face. But it is what it is.

I was not able to disconnect myself from the trauma that held me in a stagnant place, wishing things would've worked with Hobbs since we'd shared so much together. In the midst of my instability, I broke up with the other man. Instant guilt, instant regret from the pain I caused him from my unstable emotions, actions, and decisions. Let's be honest, I was not proud of myself, and I was not making the best choices to change things. I was spiraling and bringing others down with me.

Meanwhile, Hobbs had been in constant transition and was battling his own demons. After reconnecting once again, we started talking. Then we started dating again. After asking him to move in, for a very brief time, I grew frustrated beyond control with his lack of motivation or even his active presence in living. What I mean is, he was in such a dark place, feeling hopeless. He was exhausted from the crap that the Army and VA had put him through and continued to put him through daily. By that point, he felt he had nothing else to give them. On top of all that madness, he'd been on a roller coaster of over thirty surgeries, including a bone graft then implanting metal rods into the bone graft to allow his new teeth to snap in and secure into place.

He sometimes saw a doctor for counseling. He had formed a great relationship with him, and he liked to remind me of all the shitty things I'd done that he told his doctor about.

His lack of hope and appreciation for what he had ticked me off. I couldn't relate to him, and he couldn't relate to me. I thought there was a lot left to live for, and it frustrated me that he had no hope or enjoyment in life. I couldn't live like that.

Looking back on that, I realize those weren't unreasonable feelings on my part. However, no one was on his roller coaster with him and could never relate to what he was going through. Clearly, post-traumatic stress was impacting our lives. I couldn't handle it. I didn't see the hope anymore, and I ended things with Hobbs. Again.

15

THE BOY WHO CHANGED MY LIFE

Hobbs:

There I was, again, in an all-too-familiar situation, alone and abandoned. Just as I had felt for the past few years, I was back to being solo in the shitty med hold life I'd been living. *This is trash! I don't deserve this. Or do I?*

I had nothing to live for except for her. Well, that's what I thought. I was trying to show her how I felt. I wined and dined her. I took her on rides on the motorcycle. There was no one else, wasn't that enough? I was ready to marry her! I almost asked her one night. We were driving in my car on a country road as my feelings overcame me, and I was ready to propose. I wanted to but struggled to just spit it out. I didn't. Afraid of being hurt again, I let the moment pass me by.

Then she moved down south of the state for college. She was only one hour away from me before, forty-five minutes on a good day, now headed even farther away. I visited often. She was on my drive between my house and Fort Knox. I probably reported more to Fort Knox than I ever would have otherwise since I had a reason to head that way.

She asked me to live with her. I finally felt like maybe I had her heart. She loved me. She wanted me with her at all times, or so I thought.

Things changed quickly and were short-lived. Next thing I knew, we were doing it again. *She* was doing it again. Breaking up with me, claiming some bullshit about not wanting to live together. She said I needed to figure some things out. *Tramp, you need to figure out what you want, because apparently, it's not me.*

I packed my shit I had literally just moved in and returned to my house where I lived with a childhood friend, Doug. I quickly started to enjoy motorcycle life and recreational living again, including other forms of recreation, if you know what I mean. These are the years I'm not proud of. I started going on a bunch of motorcycle rides. It was a relief to just ride and try to forget everything. Granted, my bike was a piece of shit and always broke down on me.

What good was left? That was my mindset. I would've been better off if all this hadn't happened to me. If I hadn't deployed with the 1544th, I probably would've done some time. I might have gotten some sweet-ass tats, but at least I wouldn't have been blown up. I wouldn't have had to deal with all the bullshit from the Army and VA, and hey, I'd still have my teeth.

So, you're going to be a dad? A basic, yet so complicated text came in from one of my sisters after a long night of riding and staying up late working on motorcycles.

Apparently, Denise, a girl I'd had very few relations with, posted on her Myspace page, "Ryan and I are having a baby."

I called Denise and questioned her about her Myspace post. She claimed she took a home pregnancy test. I made her go to the nearby clinic with me to have a test because I just couldn't believe it. The nurse came back in after the test and confirmed the positive test. There I was sweating in the room with the results staring at me. I was in complete shock while Denise was happy and clearly excited.

Stunned and in denial, I took her home and spent the months of her pregnancy trying to ignore the situation as much as I could. I didn't even want to think about it. It was easier to live in denial than to accept reality.

The day I told my mom that I was going to have a baby she smiled with instant excitement and responded, "That's wonderful! Are Jennifer's parents excited?" Instant pain ... instant and deep. That wasn't how things were supposed to happen.

Denise didn't have a driver's license, so I took her to all her appointments. In the last few months of her pregnancy, I moved her into the house I was living in with my roommate.

October 14th, I was out on the lake fishing with a friend when Denise called. She said she was in labor. *Great, time for one more cast.* Still in denial about what was about to happen, I cast one more time.

When I arrived to pick her up to go to the hospital, it was obvious she was in labor. I could see her breathing hard and clearly in pain.

Shit.

We got in the car, and I flew to get her to the hospital. I was halfway through the city going 55 mph over an overpass on a 35-mph road when I saw an officer at the bottom of the overpass posted up on a bucket. Then I saw seven squad cars parked nearby. Clearly a speed trap. Then cherries and berries lit up in my rearview mirror.

Oh, this is awesome. I'm getting pulled over. She's going to have this baby in a car. Panicking, I got out of the car with my hands in the air saying, "I'm having a kid." They yelled for me to get back in my car. They approached the vehicle and took my license. They gave it back almost immediately when they saw Denise and verified my claim that she was having a baby.

"Turn on your flashers, we've called you in, make it there safely," the officer urged.

I was so relieved since I wasn't driving legally. I transferred the plates from another vehicle to this one. They were legal plates; I just took the initiative to do the transfer myself. I was just saving the State of Illinois some time. You're welcome, Illinois.

From the time we arrived at the hospital until the moment I first saw my son, time flew. I was still filling out paperwork in the same procedure room she was having a C-section across from me. I literally still had fish guts on my hand as I fumbled through the paperwork. My hands were shaking, and I was scared shitless.

The cries of a little baby stopped me, and my heart grew a little, kind of like the Grinch. I lifted my head from the paper-work, and there he was. My baby boy.

Doubt of him being my kid left instantly. He is definitely my son. There was no denying that Hobbs red hair. I couldn't take my eyes off him. Things got real, real fast! I just stepped into a whole new reality. A reality I'd tried to deny and had not prepared myself for. A week later, I purchased my first home. That wasn't the way things were supposed to be. I wasn't supposed to be moving my baby mama into the house I had to purchase on a whim, but I also hadn't felt any glimmer of hope in a long time. So, whether it was the plan or not, the hope my son gave me was enough.

16

THE TEXT THAT CHANGED IT ALL

JEN:

FAKE IT TILL you make it, right?

I felt like that was what I was doing—trying to stay afloat in life. I was a full-time college student, and I maintained a home with a pet and all other daily-life responsibilities. I was also working a job at a secondary transitional private school program. That opportunity helped ground me and reminded me of who I'd always wanted to be. I wanted to make a difference. I knew I had a purpose I had yet to tap into.

In the moments when I felt like things were spiraling and nothing was what I expected it would be, I tried to lie to myself. I was doing great things in my life. I was helping others at my job and finishing up my degree. I was doing well, right? I was making progress ... or so I told myself.

Honestly, I didn't even realize how much I'd lost myself. The person I was prior to the deployment hadn't returned, and I don't think she ever will. I was a different person. I disconnected myself from family and friends, got wrapped up in the hot mess I called my life. I recognized that I had things I needed to deal with, and I clearly hadn't succeeded on my own.

I decided to seek counseling and see if the VA could help me. I'd had some good experiences with the VA, some not so good, and others were terrible. I'd heard ridiculous stories from Hobbs and other battle buddies that made me sick. With apprehension in my bones, I tried to be open-minded to get the help I needed.

Is this for me? Is this going to work? I've already tried this.

The counselor seemed kind, and after the first few appointments, we dove into a process she wanted me to try. We chatted about some things during our meetings, mostly focused on how I was doing at that point, on life in general. Then, she sent me off with my first assignment. She wanted me to dig deep and write about the worst memory from my deployment. She told me to think of what was causing so much of what I was feeling. She wanted me to find the source of my feelings of sadness, regret, guilt, and helplessness.

It had been three years since that horrible experience, and I was terrified to go there. But, like I said, I knew something needed to change. So, I did it. In the privacy of my home, digging deep, listening to music, drinking some wine, and reliving those feelings, I wrote, and I wrote. The tears flowed. They were not comfortable and certainly not pretty.

I returned to the next appointment, feeling accomplished. I actually did what she expected me to. It was hard doing it, but it did seem to give me some release or some connection with what I'd tried to disconnect myself from. This disconnection and not wanting to revisit those feelings, thoughts, and memories is common when it comes to trauma.

Then the hardest part came. Holy moly, I wasn't even expecting it.

"Now that you've had the opportunity to do this exercise and really pour that out onto paper, I would like you to read it aloud," the doctor said calmly. Clearly the look on her face was more wonder than expectation. Head tilted to the side yet seemingly caring, she did not know how I would handle this and waited for my response.

Oh boy, Doc! A little heads-up would've been nice. However, I realize now that it would have defeated the purpose. In the end, it was the beginning of what I needed for my healing.

Completing all the exercises she walked me through during this healing process allowed me to confront and speak aloud what I had buried oh so deep. Definitely not a comfortable situation to dig up so many complicated, deep emotions.

Digging up those memories and emotions helped me to confront so much. I had to face my pain, confusion, and guilt. This was a turning point where I felt like I could start identifying how certain emotions were connected to certain triggers. I started to understand how I'd been feeling and why I did the things I did. I tried to grow. I was still imperfect and used destructive coping mechanisms. Yet, I tried to keep it together enough to maintain all my expected responsibilities. I mean, at least I thought so. I could do better, a lot better.

As I started to heal and I was *still* trying to find myself again, I met an amazing friend, Tiny. We quickly became friends and had a lot in common. We loved music, alcohol, God, and we didn't like idiots. We shared stories of our past. He was a riot! He told me stories of driving the bus for Cheap Trick, singing with The Marshall Tucker Band, and so much more. He was my homie, and our friendship came exactly when I needed it most.

I was finishing up school, dating a few losers, but keeping it together with the hope that the mess would get better. I had to hang onto that hope. I was trying to figure out how to get out of this dumb relationship I'd gotten myself into. Hobbs was probably back seeing that chick he had run into when we were on and off. He still texted me from time to time, usually trying to make me feel horrible for ending things with him or ignoring him.

I mean, I was not a pretty me. I did blow him off. He missed that train, remember? He wouldn't get it together when I wanted him to, so what did he expect me to do?

I was not at the best point in my life. As a matter of fact, this was one of the worst periods in my life, if not *the* worst. I was self-medicating with alcohol, spending, eating, and using other defensive coping mechanisms to bury everything.

One of the few things I enjoyed were conversations with Tiny. He kept me grounded a bit. He loved God and life as much as I did. We attended church together a few Sundays. For my birthday he gave me a purple Bible with my name engraved on it, a gift I'll forever treasure.

Tiny didn't judge me for the messy choices I made even if he didn't agree. He also didn't think I should waste my time on the loser dude I was seeing. He continued to support me as I set goals for what would come after I graduated from college. I had a hard time focusing on my goals and dreams because what I needed to do was ditch the lame boyfriend.

Trying to get it together on this freight train called life, a random text came in from Hobbs. My heart skipped a beat, and I fumbled to unlock my phone using my passcode.

I inhaled deep and opened the text. A short text, yet so life-changing: *I'm going to be a dad.*

My breath didn't return for a few moments, then I had a painful gulp deep in my throat. I stopped in my tracks realizing how the horrific results of our deployment had caught up to me. *Horrific* ... I know. It sounds harsh. It's how it felt. Hobbs was going to be a dad. A father. He was going to be a father to a child of another woman.

That was a huge turning point in my life. One I didn't handle with grace. When you get wrapped up in your own life, with your own problems, troubles, and changes, you may lose yourself a bit. Sometimes in the midst of the struggles, you forget who you are and who you want to be. You may even lie to yourself and think you got it together.

Dad? He's going to be a dad.

The words played over and over like a broken record in my head that I couldn't stop. Dumbfounded and numb, I couldn't move. Five years and this was what it had come to. Time to move on, time to figure out the future without him. I did this to myself.

17

THE START OF A SHIT SHOW

Hobbs:

Life changed drastically for me after meeting my son. This may not have been the way I wanted things to be, but I tried to look past that and not let it tear me down. After I purchased my first home, all the money that Jen and I had originally planned on using to build the house was drained into the garage I built on to the property. I also spent it on valuable essentials, most of which were not valuable or essential. Spending was a coping mechanism for me after returning from the deployment.

I was still on med hold and unable to work, living the aftermath. Over a year went by before the Army finally retired me and released me from med hold. Free at last!

I secured a factory job. This was a crazy transition for me from the last few years spent filling my time with surgeries, paperwork, avoiding paperwork, avoiding phone calls—basically avoiding all of it. Not facing reality and living in a state of denial was more my style of coping.

Life went on. Denise and I lived together, but it felt more like we were roommates. She wanted more from me, wanted me to give a shit. I mean, I was being a father and working to provide for my family. Wasn't that enough?

I blew her off and didn't want to even deal with it. I wasn't nice. I can admit that. I did what I could, and I felt like that was enough. I was doing my fatherly duties, being a dad, stepdad, and a provider. To me, that was all I owed her. The troubling thing was, what I owed to my son and stepson was more, and I knew that. I didn't want to be that kind of role model for them.

Even though I had given up my destructive lifestyle that I was living prior to the birth of my son, I still disregarded things I didn't want to deal with.

Even though I was retired from the Army, I continued to deal with their VA madness. Surgeries, appointments, and mountains of paperwork never stopped. Bills the VA failed to pay came my way. Trying to handle the situation with numerous phone calls and transfers, I got nowhere. It was a shit show. It was more than I could handle with all the various routes and connections that they wanted me to do as a result of their dropping the ball on paying for my bills. I put it in the disregard pile of bullshit that was building up.

I was so over dealing with their crap. Then a collections notice arrived after numerous phone calls and my refusing to pay for my surgery.

How completely jacked up is that? Combat vet pays bills for a crushed face caused during active duty status? Well, it was happening.

The sad thing is, I would bet the bottom half of my jaw that I'm not the only injured-in-action combat vet this has happened to. Some have stories of their experiences and the shady crap they have endured from the system—stories far worse than mine. All this after the trauma they went through and sustain for a lifetime.

Times were not easy during that period of my life, but at least I had some purpose. I had people who depended on me and a son who filled my life with a taste of the joy I'd been missing for so long. My stepson taught me so much more than I ever expected. I'm honored to be his stepdad.

I loved the boys and didn't want to let them down, but I was just waiting for an out. How could I escape it? What was my outlet? The time would come, I just knew it. So, I waited … and I waited, going through the motions, day by day. I was over it. I was over playing the part that I thought I was expected to play or the person some expected me to be.

For years, I'd done what I needed to do. I'm not saying I regretted all my decisions, by any means. But life was still painful, and it shouldn't feel like that. I learned a lot about myself over the last four years. I finally told Denise she needed to move out. Of course, she completely refused.

This happened a few more times, then finally, my breaking point. I left my own home since she refused to leave. I went to my mom's house. Denise still refused to leave, and I wasn't able to see my son. Things got uglier when I served her with an eviction notice.

Things took quite a turn when she went through a rough time. Lame for her, yet perfect timing for me. I was able to get full custody of my son and get my house back.

18

CELEBRATE THE STRUGGLE

JEN:

AFTER I GOT Hobbs's text, I sank to my lowest point. It may not have been obvious to other people, but I knew what I expected of myself. That was not it. I was not living life. I was only surviving.

I wrapped up my bachelor's degree and got a second side gig helping a woman who was navigating life in a wheelchair as a result of a car accident in her twenties. Suzie was so awesome and was exactly what I needed to add richness to my life during that time. I started to find myself a little more every day. Luckily, I'd never completely lost myself. I'd always known who I wanted to be. Hope was all I needed.

I enjoyed spending time with her even if some of my job duties stressed me out. Her spending was out of control, especially her love for late-night infomercials. She wasn't so fond of my concern about her finances, but she loved being taken out of the house to go to Kroger or Walmart followed by dinner at a fast-food restaurant of her choice. Most of the time her dinner choice depended on what coupons she had scored that week.

As I was faced with the decision on what to do after college, it wasn't a hard decision. I had to go home and ditch the boyfriend. But I didn't get the nerve to dump him before I headed back to my hometown, and he came with me! I was such a coward and *still* couldn't tell him to just stop. I moved home, stayed with my parents while I immediately started looking for a house. A few months later I bought my first home and worked a full-time job at a daycare.

I secured the house and paid for his U-Haul to go back home. Deuces, peace out, Boy Scout! This is no exaggeration: I was just hoping he would return the U-Haul once he made it home since it was in my name. Fortunately, he did, and I never had to hear from him again.

Alone, finally, I was in my own home, ready to pick up the pieces called my life. Praise Jesus! My best friend Kelli moved in. Best roomie ever! She helped me navigate through that transition in my life. My healing and growth continued. Happiness revisited my life for the first time in a long time. Like pure happiness that felt familiar yet so foreign, and I hadn't felt it in a long time. A long, long time.

Kelli and I shared so much of our time together even though we worked different shifts. She worked long hours in a cath lab; meanwhile I got my first special education teaching job in a third through fifth grade classroom for students with behavioral and emotional needs.

Life got easier and more hope came to my life as I reconnected with family and friends. I started dating an old high school friend who happened to be Kelli's cousin. He moved in with Kelli and me. So together, we lived life. We laughed together, grew together, and learned together.

Three years into our relationship, I was on a trip to Colorado with my Army girls, celebrating Cawvey Day, October 6th, chatting it up with my fellow battle buddies.

I started to vent, "Man, I just don't feel like this is a good relationship I'm in. We aren't on the same page."

Instantly, one of my homies turned and looked at me; she was standing two feet from me. She tilted her chin with sadness and empathy and said, "Aww, Buff, you said that a year ago."

Whoa, um, what? Stop it! Stop calling me out on my faults I'm not ready to accept let alone recognize. Crap! That was a defining moment, and I never saw it coming.

I returned home after my girls' trip and the perfect God-sent gift came my way: an invite to a women's Bible study on the book of James. At the time, I didn't see it as God-sent. I was trying to do something to move toward the person I'd always known myself and my soul to be. A student, always learning, a child of God, always serving, and then of course ... always growing, yet still imperfect.

It didn't take long for the words to speak to me. Right away these words shifted my whole thinking and my universe:

"Consider it pure joy, my brothers, whenever you face trials of many kinds. Because you know that the testing of your faith develops perseverance." James 1:2

It was okay to have those trials; it was even more valuable. You gained a deeper appreciation for life. This awakening in my life was so life-changing for me, but it led me to hurt another person. Another person I loved and truly cared about.

In a conversation with my brother, he asked me, "How do you do it?"

My dumb response: "Do what?"

"Just walk away from relationships, break up, and be okay with it?" he questioned with complete puzzlement.

Oh, my goodness. Excuse me while I hang my head low, oh so low.

That ... that was what my big brother thought of me. That was what he saw from my actions, so of course, that was what he thought of me. I wished I could say aloud, "The outside of me is not what I look like on the inside."

Regardless of how I looked or how I was perceived by others, I broke up with my boyfriend after three years. I could say a lot right here. I could talk about how hard the end was or the lack of connection prior, but I won't. I will say this: my favorite story about his kind soul is how he gathered up a Thanksgiving plate one holiday and drove it out to a homeless person sitting outside a local grocery store. Though he may have been absent in our relationship, he was a servant to others.

The breakup wasn't an easy one, and of course, I drew a great deal of attention to myself as anyone would breaking up with someone after three years without some obvious, significant event that caused it. Some understood, others had trouble understanding, as I expected.

Adding fuel to the fire, I engaged in a relationship shortly after the breakup when Hobbs asked me on a date. It was completely random on the timing of him messaging me. Sounds sketchy, yes, I know. But he had just broken up with his baby mama and decided to message me. I hesitated, but I thought, *I lost him once. I'm not going to lose him again. It's all or nothing.*

I am human. I am full of faults and sin. I am given grace. How ugly would we see ourselves if we didn't give ourselves grace? I had a lot of growing to do. God was not through with me yet. He had plans for me, and I was going to figure it out.

Kelli had been there for me during my transition back to my hometown. She was my life coach, counselor, and best friend. She bought her own home and moved out. It may have been because of the chore list I had created. Ha-ha! Not really, but we enjoy laughing about that.

I didn't know the crap Hobbs had been through over the previous five years. I caught a glimpse of it though. One weekend, I went with him to Rock Island to check in with whomever he had to go see. He was constantly being sent here, there, everywhere.

We made it to the building where we were surrounded by brass, meaning everyone was an officer. From colonels to lieutenants, they were everywhere. I was in civilian clothes and Hobbs was back in the ol' BDUs. As we walked to the office, passing by all the brass, one soldier, the *only* soldier not rocking officer rank, stopped Hobbs. This guy was literally the same rank as both Hobbs and me, an E-4 Specialist. He pointed at Hobbs's nametags on his chest and said, "Hey Specialist, your tags are on the wrong side."

In classy Hobbs fashion, he looked down, ripped the tags from their Velcro and swapped them around. He glanced up at the E-4 and said, "Ha-ha, oh, thanks." I was holding back my laughter, as I was about to lose it. That joker had some balls. Maybe he didn't see Hobbs's face and busted up jaw, maybe he did. Either way, the amusement it gave us that morning was unforgettable.

Hobbs is a medical mystery turned medical miracle. The doctors did an insane job rebuilding his upper jaw, implanting metal posts, and giving him a set of teeth almost identical to his real ones.

Apparently, I wasn't the only one impressed with the work they'd done. He was invited to be a guest speaker at a Biomedical Research Convention. The doctors there had been studying how to clone or produce bone without having to do bone grafts, like Hobbs had done.

When he arrived, he thought he was going to have to speak

to a room of no more than twenty people or so. He found out quickly that he was so wrong. He called me and told me how he was staying at a grand hotel, and the auditorium was full of hundreds of doctors. I couldn't help but laugh because I knew that was so not his cup of tea. He survived though and made a lot of connections there.

Back home, I decided to list my house with a local realtor because I was ready to shed and release it all. My house sold in just two months, and I was excited to move in with Kelli at her new home. She invited me in and allowed me to live there while I figured out my next step, which quickly became clear.

One day Kelli and I were doing what we enjoyed most—binge watching trash TV—because we were trapped in the house with half a foot of snow. It was too high for our vehicles to conquer. Unexpectedly, a friend of ours came by and plowed the driveway for us. So, Kelli and I got out and met up with her dad at a local restaurant for gyros.

We finished our delicious meal and drove home. Within five minutes of being home, I started to feel absolutely terrible. I was dizzy and nauseous. I lay down in bed sweating bullets. Kelli was concerned but had to leave for work. She brought me a glass of water and a trash can and left me alone as I had requested in my miserable state.

After an hour or so I pulled it together enough to get up out of bed. Kelli left for work, and I was ready to relax. I saw the Pink Moscato in the fridge and poured myself a glass of wine before sitting down to binge watch television. It wasn't the same without my roomie, but I was still excited.

On a commercial break I headed for the bathroom. Even though I knew my period was about to start any day, I decided to take a pregnancy test that was sitting in the cabinets. I have no idea what made me do it. I finished up and set the stick on the sink. I wasn't even done washing my hands before the line of pink the same color of my wine showed up in the danger zone on the stick. What the—?

What just happened? Is this a joke? Cameras!! Where are they? This is seriously a joke.

Beside myself, I was smiling yet confused and scared at the same time. A baby? What?! Me ... a mom?!

I stood there, dumbfounded. I looked at my wine glass, hesitated, then dumped it out in the sink. *I dumped my wine out.* Suddenly my mind was racing. What would I do since I worked with students with behavioral needs? I hoped that wouldn't affect this possible baby. *Holy cow, did I just say that? A baby!!! Somebody fill my wine back up!*

I made a trip the next night to surprise Hobbs with the shocking, but good news. He was just as shocked as I was. We'd been together only a few months. At the end of the school year, we celebrated with family and friends the reveal of the baby's gender. A girl! A perfect baby girl.

Hobbs, his son, and I, with a baby in my belly, scheduled our first mini getaway together. We planned to go to an indoor water park during the summer. On the day we were packing up to leave, Hobbs hollered to me from the living room. I was busy packing in the bedroom.

"What? I'm packing," I hollered back.

"Jen, come here," he said again.

A bit annoyed and impatient to go on the trip, I headed to the living room to see what he was hollering about.

In the center of the living room, Hobbs and his son were down on one knee, holding out a ring, wearing ecstatic smiles, and had one simple question.

"Will you marry us?" they asked in unison.

Though it may not have been a simple question five years ago, this time, it was simple.

Overjoyed, I answered, "Yes, yes, yes!"

The hardest job I've ever had is being a mother. Don't get me wrong, I love the job. I am grateful and thankful for the honorary role. It certainly is the most confusing, strenuous, fulfilling, and defeating role thus far.

Prior to giving birth to my daughter, my stepson taught me how to be a mom. My mother also had a lot to do with that. But until I was actually "in the trenches," I didn't have a clue just how demanding being a parent was. Fortunately for me, I had an amazing little human to help guide me on my new path.

The transition into the role as stepmom wasn't exactly smooth sailing. You could only imagine. The fact was, life changed significantly for all of us, including Denise. It wasn't easy for any of us, and at times, it was downright rough.

After a bit of hate mail we received to our house, threatening us and our unborn child with wild accusations, I was full of anger. I felt completely violated. The fact that an unknown someone would violate our privacy with so much disrespect as to send a threatening letter to my home—that dug up feelings I hadn't felt in years since my deployment. It felt like an attack, and I was left trying to figure out how to deal with it. I had to work through that period of my life, pregnant. Since I had up and moved from my hometown, I was living in Hobbs's hometown. Hardly anyone knew me except him.

As I worked through those emotions, I knew the letter had to have been on behalf of Denise. It could've been planned and carried out by her or not. Either way, it didn't feel good.

Then, I took a step back and saw the situation from a different perspective. From her point of view, she was losing the life she wanted with Hobbs and her boys. That anger and pain could make people do dumb stuff. So, whether it was her or not, I needed to figure out how to express myself clearly and do what was best for my stepson.

A few months after the hate mail, I approached Denise at a T-ball game. I asked her if we could chat, and she obliged.

Doing the best I could to be real and stay true to myself, I began, "Look, I want you to know that I am very thankful to be in your son's life. I realize things haven't been easy. I want you to know though, that I am not trying to take your spot. You are his mother, and it's wonderful that you are a part of his life. I would never try to take your place."

A bit surprised and taken aback, she kindly replied, "Well thank you, I appreciate you telling me that."

Over the years it wasn't easy with us all co-parenting together, but I would be lying if I said things hadn't gotten better. I think for all of us, we have all learned and grown from life with struggles and celebrations. Having extended families can be challenging, but holy cow, it is certainly beautiful as well. I for one, feel blessed to have extended family.

After the birth of our first daughter, we got married on October 4, 2014. I'd always imagined having a fall wedding, and I thought that if we put it right around "Cawvey Day," aka Hobbs's "Alive Day," then it would be something joyful to look forward to during that hard time of the year.

Many of our friends and family came to see us get married, including a bunch of our battle buddies. Everyone seemed to be as excited to see us tie the knot as we were.

Things for Hobbs and me were still a work in progress. Our love was strong, yet we both still struggled with our own demons. We sought out counseling to help work through some of our issues with the same doctor he saw when he returned from Iraq.

Doctor Lee was thrilled to see things come full circle and to see that we had reunited. He listened and understood both of us more than we sometimes understood ourselves. He taught us tolerance and how to listen more to one another. He reminded us that we were quite a team, and together, we would persevere through the struggles. He was right. It is not all pretty with love and marriage. It takes work, patience, and the willingness to meet your partner in the middle.

19

JEN'S BACK

Hobbs:

SOMEBODY PINCH ME—SURELY *I'm dreaming. This is crazy.*

I was living a life that I was reluctant to start. I love my son and stepson, but that wasn't the life I had planned or hoped for. I appreciated the things I had, and the boys gave me a purpose to live and strive for more. It took me completely by surprise when Jen actually responded to my messages. She seemed different because I was so used to her blowing me off and being super short with me. I mean, I guess I get it. Only somewhat though. I was good at pressing my luck and continued to text her, engaging in a bit of flirtation because that's what I do best —push the limits.

Even though we hadn't talked in a while, I expected her to message me back. She owed it to me, or at least I thought so. I didn't even know what to think most of the time. All those emotions were hard to comprehend and face. Dealing with reality was much harder than living in a denial state. I had relished in that for quite some time.

I heard from my sister, and she told me that Jen had broken up with her boyfriend. Which one? I didn't know. Who could keep up with her and her many boyfriends? I just knew it wasn't me. Although, I wished it were. That feeling had never gone away. I loved her so much it hurt.

Although my son had been such a blessing and refilled my soul with love I'd never known, there was still that missing piece. That piece that I didn't feel whole without. So, why waste any time? Recent breakup or not, I asked Jen on a date.

She accepted, and the rest is history. Well, it's not exactly history because it isn't over. History continues to be made daily. So, yes, it wasn't the happily ever after I was expecting, but it was a dream coming to life. Our dates grew more frequent, and our love grew significantly. I guess I wasn't expecting that. I knew our love was strong, but I never imagined this ... now ... with the current circumstances and the past struggles.

She lived almost two hours away from me, so it wasn't easy for us to see each other daily, but we certainly tried to see each other weekly. Jen met my son and they quickly enjoyed one another. The transition of seeing a new female in the house wasn't easy for him. The hardest part was when he would come back to my house from visiting his mom. That was when he was emotional and got super upset, sometimes crying and throwing fits. From time to time, he would ask if he could live with her. It was hard to see him sad. I felt bad that he had to go through those feelings of separation.

Those were the greatest feelings of pain that I would say I don't necessarily regret, but certainly didn't intend. It was rough, and I would think, *I wasn't made for this*. I wasn't made to cause pain. I only knew how to deal with things with humor. Remembering who I was helped me get through the craziness.

Although I continued to work in the civilian world, I constantly had to go to appointments to maintain the work I'd had done. Doctors made training videos, using me as the example. They invited me to speak at a Biomedical Research Convention. They wanted to pay for my flight, hotel room, and all my meals if I was willing to speak at the convention.

Free trip? I obliged and headed out to the conference. My understanding was that I would have to speak to a room of doctors, about twenty or so, I thought. Holy hell was I wrong! It was a freaking auditorium. Every seat was packed, some were even standing at the back. I estimated there were at least three hundred doctors there. The rest was a blur. They asked me questions; I answered, but it felt like a complete out-of-body experience.

One February evening, Jen made a random trip to my house to have dinner which was surprising because she had to work the next day. She played with my son and our dog, Tyson. Tyson was originally her dog that I got for her. Trying to share him and move him back and forth caused Tyson to feel protective and confused. Because of that, I kept him during the five years we were apart.

She made a chocolate cake for dessert. My son helped her to stir and lick the bowl. As he was in the other room and she was about to serve it, she said we were celebrating. I looked at her, confused, trying to figure out what she was talking about. She said we were celebrating a birthday or something like that. Still puzzled, I was smiling, still trying to figure it out. She then told me that we were having a baby.

Yes, yes, yes, yes! I got her trapped now. Ha!

Elated with joy, I scooped her up and hugged her so tight. We decided to keep it to ourselves for the time being.

YES! THIS! This was exactly everything I had always wanted. Jen and I were going to have a baby. My son was going to be a big brother.

20

TRIGGERED

JEN:

IT WASN'T EXACTLY a typical Saturday morning at the Hobbs house since we had been off for three days for Thanksgiving break. This Saturday was different; we had an invitation to walk in a parade with some of our fellow battle buddies and their families. The problem was, we thought it was okay to start drinking early.

Now, I'm not proud of my actions, and frankly, I'm a bit embarrassed. You see, the truth is, I'm not sure what made me want to start drinking mimosas on a Saturday morning when I knew I had to be in a parade at 6:30 p.m. to stand proud with the fellow veterans I served with. I don't know for sure why I would do that.

I do, however, have a few ideas. I always have anxiety and panic before I go to see my fellow battle buddies. It's weird. I love them and completely enjoy the company of most of them, but I guess their presence in my life does trigger deep feelings. I don't do well under pressure. I use drinking as a coping mechanism, and it needs to be dealt with and controlled. Finally, I can be honest with myself and accept my faults. Only when I accept my faults can I grow from them.

The parade was a success. We hit up some food trucks and headed to the brewery we met Johns and her family at before the parade.

Shitty turning point ... Hobbs had too much to drink, and the band gave a shout-out to our unit that we served with in Iraq. Now, I don't know if it was the alcohol, the choice of the song, or both, but when they started playing "Wish You Were Here," everything turned a bit south. If you recall, this is the same song in Cawvey's memorial slideshow.

A fellow vet, not from our unit, could see the anguish on Hobbs's face. When Hobbs was in the bathroom, he approached me.

"Hey, my name is Josh. I can see your husband is having a hard time. I'd like to buy him a drink," he said.

I could see the man had only one leg, and I asked him, "Are you a veteran as well?"

"Yes, but I didn't experience combat," he said.

"Well thank you for asking, but I'm not exactly sure about the drink. That song that just played dug deep and reminded him of our battle buddy that died in the truck he was in when they were hit by a roadside bomb. Usually he probably would appreciate it, but I think he's struggling right now," I responded.

"I understand. Thanks for the heads-up." He walked away, and I saw him visit Hobbs at the bar as he was getting a drink. It must've gone okay, because next thing I knew, they were chatting it up.

As I was taking in the quality rhythms of the band, I told Johns it was probably time for me to go round up my husband for departure. I carefully approached the bar as I scanned the situation. Something seemed off. I inched up to a vacant spot at the bar; the bartenders were whispering to each other, glaring at my husband. They were clearly mean mugging him. What was going on? I looked at Hobbs and saw him glaring right back at the bartenders with a pissed off expression. One of the bartenders handed him his fresh beer, a glass of water, and a small bowl of snacks.

Then something snapped, and Hobbs threw up two middle fingers to the bartenders, "You don't know me. My buddy Shaun and I will come up in here with guns!" He was shouting and looking like he was about to pounce over the bar.

Oh my! No, he did not just say that! Hobbs was so not like this. I was so confused as to what had just transpired. I didn't waste any time trying to figure it out. I immediately started trying to get him to make his way to the door, placing myself between him and all the bartenders so he could potentially see or hear me.

"Come on Ryan, let's go. Time to go home. Calm down. Listen to me. Let's go," I said as I took his arm in mine and made our way to the exit. Luckily, he stopped mouthing off until we got outside. Johns followed us out and walked with us to the car. She was cool, calm, and collected, whereas I felt frustrated. That wasn't cool, and it wasn't the way I wanted to end the night. It was a struggle to get to the car with my vicious pit bull. Hobbs attempted to get in the driver seat, and I took the keys from him.

"Absolutely not, Ryan. You are drunk. I'm driving," I said adamantly. He didn't take well to that and was trying to get in as cars were driving right by us on the road we were parked on the side of. He finally got in the passenger's seat. I was scared. I didn't know what was going to happen. I had never seen him like this.

Fortunately, he passed out before we made it out of town. Bad thoughts went through my mind the whole hour-and-a-half ride home. *What if I just drove off the side of the road?* I could see why people sometimes felt like that was an easier option. Dealing with grief and trauma is a struggle.

I pulled into the driveway of our home, and I couldn't wake Hobbs. I tried to get him out of the car, and he just lay down on the driveway. I considered leaving him there, but since it was wintertime and probably not a good idea to leave him passed out for all to see, I didn't give up. I finally got him inside and felt a sense of relief. What a confusing night!

The conversation the next day was not easy. Hobbs knew things didn't end well. He could remember that. He told me about what had happened prior to me walking up to him at the bar. Apparently, another nearby stranger overheard his war stories and started talking shit about the National Guard being weekend warriors and some other crap.

I was super upset by Hobbs's actions that night, and we had to work through the growth we identified that we needed. Once I heard what his trigger was, it did help to shed some light on the crazy situation. People don't realize what ignorant comments can do and how much they can trigger in someone. A combat veteran has warrior reflexes that they have been trained to use. His reflex was to become defensive and to protect himself, even if it was triggered from someone's lousy choice of words.

21

TELL ME I AM DREAMING

Hobbs:

Jen always talks me into doing things I don't want to do. I'm not a big fan of crowds and get uncomfortable outside of my comfort zone. Somehow though, she convinces me to go there, to step outside of my box and do things I feel I can't do. With her by my side, it's easier.

She convinced me to attend a formal veterans' dinner. Excited to have a night alone, without kids, we decided to walk across the street for a few beers after the banquet.

Jen and I sat at the end of the bar, listening to the music, people watching, and chatting. We talked to another veteran, Conner, who was also at the dinner. We discovered he was a service officer for the VA. Jen told him about all I'd been through with the VA and the bills I'd paid from my surgeries. He was shocked, but I was so used to that mess. That was old news.

I stopped going to the VA for my maintenance plan for my

bone graft. Those sorry bastards didn't want to follow through with the plan of treatment they'd started with and wanted to jack my shit all up. The doc felt it would be more manageable for them if they just pulled all my metal implanted posts out and gave me dentures.

Conner was horrified by what he heard as I explained what I had been through in the past decade. He handed us his card and encouraged us to get a hold of him. Jen was all about it and put the card in her pocket. She's always been like that. She felt like it was absolutely asinine and should be fixed. Whereas I felt defeated by the system; I didn't want to give it anymore of me. I'd given enough. We ended the evening and made the quick walk across the street to our hotel.

I was stopped by another vet before we reached the hotel door. We started talking, and Jen continued to the door. After a brief exchange of words, I glanced over at Jen and saw her lying on her back on the concrete. What the hell? It was the middle of winter, and snow was still on the ground.

"Jen, what are you doing?" I questioned with a confused laugh.

I approached her to figure out what in the hell she was doing. As I got closer, I saw so much blood around her head. Instant panic. The blood was coming from her ear. I just lost it. I called for help and screamed for someone to call 911.

The officers and ambulance arrived, they asked me questions about what happened and wouldn't let me go to Jen or on the ambulance. They didn't handcuff me, but they detained me to the side while they checked security footage.

You think I did this to my wife?

I was completely freaked out inside and beyond pissed off that I couldn't go to her. They shut the doors of the ambulance, and she left without me. Just then an officer walked out of the hotel and said, "He's good. She fell." They released me from their designated area. I was enraged.

The adrenaline was fierce in my blood. Conner must've seen all this transpire out the windows of the bar and came over to help calm me down. He was a hero for me that night, and I would hate to see how the night would have gone had he not been there. He drove me to the hospital where I found Jen in the emergency room. She was lying there unconscious, hooked up to so many machines. *She has to be okay. I need her to be okay!*

22

"YOU FELL AND HIT YOUR HEAD."

Jen:

I struggled to wake. As I came to and opened my eyes, I realized I was in a hospital bed. My head throbbed with pain like I'd never felt. I looked around, trying to move my head side to side. My mother-in-law and father-in-law were next to my bed. On the other side of the bed, I saw Hobbs and my brother, Scott. I was instantly confused and wanted to know what was going on. The pain was so intense that I started to moan and tried to speak. Extremely devastated on how I got there, I started asking questions and wondering why my head hurt so bad.

"Well, dear, you fell," my father-in-law told me. My mother-in-law was next to him, and I saw the concern on her face as she nodded.

I couldn't even comprehend this. I was fine.

"Fell? What do you mean I fell?" No one could really answer me. I fell? I tripped? Hit the side of my head? No one knew. Everyone assumed I hit the side of my head since I had a lot of blood loss from my ear.

I was in and out of it. Things were so foggy, but I understood it was bad since I'd been transferred from the emergency room to the intensive care unit. The doctor came in to talk to me about the different places I cracked on my skull, intracranial bleeding, and ... um ... *say what, Doc? I cracked my skull? Like the bone that protects my brain? Oh, my Dear Lord Baby Jesus, what is going on?*

I could tell things were seriously wrong. People were traveling hours to come see me. A few of my battle buddies came to visit me. I couldn't talk much, but their presence was a comfort. My mom and brother stayed most of the time.

As I gained more composure, I instantly became so sad, "Doc, am I going to be able to make my flight in a few days? I'm supposed to be a bridesmaid at my best friend's wedding."

"Dear you won't be doing a whole lot for the next few weeks. You definitely can't fly," he broke the news to me.

Tears flowed, and my heart broke a little. My mom took on the tasks of breaking the news to Kelli and canceling my flight and hotel.

"I can't believe this! I have to be there," I cried.

"It's going to be okay, Jen. You can't go. You need to recover and take care of yourself," my mother reassured me.

"Oh, my God, my students! They are going to be so worried about me. My lesson plans, they aren't ready!" I cried harder.

"I've already talked to your principal. She said she will take care of everything. She just wants you to focus on getting better," my mom told me.

Why was this happening? How did this happen? I was fine! I remembered everything ... well almost everything. Things weren't clear after we exited the bar to walk across the street to the hotel. Why couldn't I remember that? Did I trip? Slide on ice? I didn't get it!

The recovery was so rough. The pain was relentless, and in the first few weeks, the only thing I could do for relief was immerse myself into a scorching hot bath. The intense heat penetrated my pores hot like lava, and for a moment, I could take my focus from the pain at the rear base of my head. I took around four baths a day just to have some relief. I needed help dressing and getting around most of the time.

Loved ones came to visit me. The support from friends, family, and my coworkers was so humbling, to say the least. For the first few weeks, I struggled to maintain conversations or tolerate audio and visual stimulation. Everyone was so worried about me. I could tell this had triggered feelings deep within my battle buddies as well. I wasn't the only one struggling. I could tell this affected those I love.

I was so confused. I couldn't even comprehend the feelings I went through. Would I ever be okay? I tried to make sense of it all. Even to the extent that I thought maybe this was God's way of telling me to live life and stop being such a worry wart. Life was short and could be changed or taken away in the blink of an eye. I needed to stop stressing over dumb things and cherish every moment, every day.

I didn't understand what had happened. I couldn't accept it. I kept asking questions about what happened, trying to make sense of it all.

But how did I fall? Did I trip forward or backward? How can I not remember this? Because I remember the whole night. I was fine, damn it.

That was what I told myself. Honestly, I wasn't fine. Something had happened, and I had to find out so I could move on. Hobbs couldn't answer any of my questions because he didn't see it happen. He knew everything I knew ... all the way up to crossing the street before his conversation with the fellow veteran in the parking lot.

As I tried to piece things together about that night, I thought about what the police officer had said before they released my husband: "She fell." That statement was all we had to go on. That statement alone started all the assumptions, and I wanted to find out what had really happened. I needed to know because I needed some sort of closure. I needed someone to tell me that I was okay. I needed someone to confirm that I didn't have a seizure and that nothing was wrong with me that may have caused it. Was it alcohol? Was I roofied when that bartender passed over the shot I didn't pay for and told me he had poured it for someone who changed their mind? That was stupid of me. I don't even like shots. What was I thinking? Was it that?

I decided to call the hotel for some insight since I knew they had video footage where I fell just outside the door. The hotel answered, and I explained how I was there a month ago and fell outside which resulted in an emergency situation. I acknowledged that I knew it was caught on camera, and I wanted to see the video. The secretary took my name and number for the head of security to call me back. So, I waited and the next day I received a call back.

"Hi, this is Ron, head of security at the hotel. I had a message to call you back," the voice on the other end of the line stated.

"Hi, my name is Jennifer Hobbs. I was in an accident last month outside of your hotel. An ambulance was called, and I know the police on site checked the cameras. This has all been rather life-altering for me. I'm trying to process it all and figure out what happened. I was hoping I could see the video," I said anxiously.

"Well, ma'am, if you want to see the video, you have to go

through a process of paperwork to request it. I was the head of security on duty that night. I might be able to answer your questions."

I was stunned. "You were there? You saw the video?" I asked with puzzled shock. I was talking to someone who might know more than even I knew about this devastating event in my life that I'd been trying to make sense of.

"Yeah, and I have it pulled up right in front of me," he said.

Oh my gosh. My heart and head raced a thousand miles a minute.

I explained, "Well, this has all been life-changing. Which is an understatement. I just can't understand it and need to have some things cleared up. How did I fall? Did I trip forward? Did I slip on ice? Did I fall backward?"

He responded, "Actually you didn't trip at all. It's pretty strange. You are just standing there. It looks like your husband is about twenty feet away with his back to you talking to someone. Then ... you just fall backward." He stopped.

"Like ... I faint?" I questioned.

"Yeah, it's really strange. You are just standing still, then next thing you fall backward."

All those ugly puzzle pieces started coming together, making far more sense. I hadn't fainted since basic training but tended to have "episodes" near fainting. I had gotten better at identifying the feelings when they came on and always tried to prevent it by sitting down and getting a snack.

There it was. An actual explanation other than "you fell." I fainted and fell straight back onto my head. That helped to make the connection as to why the majority of the vicious pain came from the back of my head, not the side, like the ER thought. The side of my skull cracked too, but only from the force of the impact.

Now what?

A bit of closure with what happened helped me clear up some feelings of anxiety about not knowing what had happened. It was still so devastating and disappointing. How did I not feel it coming on? I was good at identifying it. Damn it! Why hadn't I sat down?

Another month of recovery at home and hoping for the best, Hobbs had to return to work since his family medical leave of absence was up with me. I was scared. Like legit scared. I am not a sissy when it comes to being home alone or doing anything independently. But my body had been doing weird things, and I was scared of being alone.

I made it through the month, and as much as I wanted to return to work, I was nervous. I wanted to be ready but didn't know if I was just trying to tell myself that. It was finally time for my follow-up neurology appointment; I'd been waiting anxiously to hear how the healing of my skull was going.

Other than pages and pages of my care plan and documents that I was sent home with from the hospital after the fall, I was in the dark with what damage I really did. All I could do was Google the ridiculous diagnoses on the paperwork from the hospital. Bleeding on the brain, closed fractures ... ugh. This wasn't happening.

At my follow-up appointment, I sat in the waiting room and the time on the clock seemed to drag. My heart raced. I had so many questions. Did I do this to myself? Was I going to be okay?

The great news, I would be okay. She reassured me that my skull should heal fine. My smell and taste may never return, or it might.

I asked tons of questions about whether I could've prevented it and if it was my fault.

The neurologist looked at me sympathetically. "Listen Jennifer, you need to grant yourself some grace. Accidents happen. I have fainted before right onto my face. I had only had one drink and was in front of all my colleagues. We could sit there and beat ourselves up and point blame, but what good is that? You are going to be okay and are healing well. Give yourself some grace."

Tears instantly started pouring. I released something I had been holding onto for two months. I needed someone to tell me that. This had been so life-shaking and scary, I needed to hear that.

So now, I felt better about what might happen, and tried to remind myself not to be afraid. I could go back to work. I could do this. I just had to listen to my body. I had already been keeping my boss up to date on my status, and she knew I was planning to return the Monday after my Friday neurology appointment. That was the plan.

Then, the COVID pandemic of 2020 ruined everything. Not only was I not going to get out of the house where I'd been for two months already, but I was now quarantined with my family *and* had to teach remotely to my beloved students I hadn't seen since before the accident.

Those four months after my accident were relentless and continued to challenge me personally. I didn't cope well and felt like things were so out of my control. I went from recovering from a head injury to teaching remotely which I'd never had to do. I was also managing remote learning at home for my two kids and my nephew. Brutal to say the least!

I received more shocking news during a virtual appointment with my endocrinologist. I'd been seeing an endocrinologist for ten years because of my thyroid issues and a benign tumor under my brain in my pituitary gland. I caught her up on the madness that had occurred and how the hotel security officer described it as fainting.

As I worked to process the reasoning for it, seeking her

input, she asked me, "Has anyone ever told you that you are in the prediabetic range?" I told her about my history and different things that had happened that left me concerned, but blood work was never brought to my attention. Together, we reflected on all the food and drinks I'd had that day, followed by a lot of evening coffee, a large meal, and carb-filled beer.

She helped me piece together what was most likely happening with my body when it was in the prediabetic range. She gave me more insight than I had received since the accident. I was beyond grateful. I must make changes to get away from this stupid prediabetic range. I need to make more than a measly effort to change my diet and to prevent anything else terrible from happening.

Yet another turning point in my life, but this time, I'm an adult. People count on me now. I have to learn how to cope with life better so that my body doesn't suffer.

So how does one do that? Well, that is the million-dollar question for some of us. I can say that it doesn't look the same for all of us. We are all different. We get satisfaction, pleasure, and love from different sources. We also deal with life's stressors differently. We are all unique and far from perfect since there is no such thing.

I hit what seemed like my rock bottom and focused on how I was going to get out of it. I decided I was going to get back to writing. Writing fills my soul and helps me to express myself. Sometimes I don't communicate the best with my words.

I dug up Conner's card that he had given us in February and emailed him to touch base and let him know that I was doing well. Delighted to hear from us, he immediately motivated us to file a claim on Hobbs's and my behalf. He seemed to care and wanted to help us resolve our issues with the VA.

For years, Hobbs and I saw others get disability ratings higher than his. It was absolutely asinine. How in the heck did they claim that he got only ten percent for his jaw? They claimed, "It doesn't affect his ability to complete daily tasks, so it is not recognized." It was apparently not on the huge list of injuries they referred to when deciding on ratings. *That's a shocker! You mean you've never had someone with their upper jaw smashed? Well, duh, idiots.*

I'm still learning and training myself to cope with things in healthier ways. I have found various healthy habits to incorporate into my life that have helped me to grow in more than just one way. I'm a fan of reading, writing, dancing, and singing. I enjoy exercising and doing other things to stay active, both indoors and outdoors. I've had to make an effort to reignite my desires and passions that used to bring more enjoyment. I miss that part of myself. I miss that appreciation for life.

Whatever it is that you use to self-regulate needs to be what is successful for you and supports your growth. In the end, your growth acts as a domino effect which results in other areas of your life having more growth and success.

THE WAR AT HOME

JEN:

I'VE HEARD the war at home can be just as hard as the actual war. Huge comparison, right? Understatement? I don't think so. Everyone has their own war. No two people experience the same war in the combat zone. Some miss the birth of their children; some will never see their children again. Our families experience their own "war" on the home front during and after. Their lives completely change when their soldier leaves for the combat zone. The absence of a child, parent, or spouse can be hell.

All soldiers have a different return home. Some come home to families, some had more family when they were on deployment and have no one to return home to. The war continues on the home front. People struggle with addictions, broken marriages, loss of loved ones, fights with disease, loss of jobs, and so much more.

It's hard enough to transition back into civilian life, let

alone deal with the stress you carry from your deployment. Some people don't like to acknowledge their service as a soldier, or they keep it a secret that they are a veteran. I've heard people say that they don't want to be judged by their military experience. The older I get and the more experience I have, the more I understand that judgment is definitely a thing. I guess I was just ignorant to this fact. Especially in the generation we live in, veterans can sometimes be doubted in the workplace due to preconceived notions about veterans. Some view us as a liability. Empathy and understanding are lacking which is a shame.

I don't have enough fingers and toes to count how many times someone has asked me if my military plates belong to my husband. Upon my return, I made a trip out to visit my birth father. On the first night of my visit, we were at a bar when he was proudly bragging to others about his daughter having just returned from a combat zone. The other civilian seemed interested and said that he was in the Army long ago as well.

Acting polite and interested, I thanked him for his service and inquired about his time in the military. Once he learned that I was in the Army National Guard, his whole demeanor changed. His tone of voice and the way he looked at me took a turn as he reminisced. "Oh yeah, I served with reserves on base as well. They would come for a few weeks and then leave to go home, while the rest of us active Army folks had to continue."

Needless to say, I didn't take well to his remarks. I quickly let him know that five of my Army National Guard buddies gave their lives for him to have the freedom to stand there and bad-mouth their service to our country. I looked him in the eye the whole time as I angrily said what I had to say. Knowing I had control of the situation, my father didn't step in. I handled it, and we walked away. Peace out ignorance!

Judgement is a real thing. These comments are ignorant

and can boil up deep feelings that we have not yet been trained to deal with.

When we learn to identify that we need to grow in certain areas, that is a pivotal point in life. You can't experience personal growth if you can't acknowledge where it is needed. It is okay to struggle; it doesn't make you any less of a person.

After a decade and a half, I am now learning more about myself than I have ever known. I think this has a lot to contribute to personal growth. I had to acknowledge and face my faults and the uncomfortable memories of myself. I think your character is built from your actions or lack thereof. If you can't identify the areas in your life that need attention and work, then you are kidding yourself. Identifying our not-so-great qualities and our weaknesses is not an easy process. It certainly isn't the most comfortable. Challenging and comfortable don't really mix. The good news is something challenging can end up changing you or your circumstances, resulting in making things more comfortable.

I have spent too long utilizing destructive coping mechanisms. "Destructive coping mechanisms are easy," and oh, so available (Falke and Goldberg 2018). The productive defense mechanisms require more work. They require training, enlightenment, and understanding on what those types of coping mechanisms are and what they look like. They are far from easy and not encouraged as much when seeking support.

I have struggled with my own issues. I have had difficulty maintaining relationships and controlling my impulsive responses. I've learned that I need to work on responding, rather than reacting. It's not an easy transition when you have been trained to use your "warrior responses" (Falke and Goldberg 2018). We have to learn on our own what responses are not appropriate for certain situations. It is an ongoing process that I believe all returning combat veterans deal with.

These responses are confusing to some. Of course, they are. I mean how many people do you know who jump at a sound behind them or freak out from fireworks? How many people do you know who expect the personal space around them to be respected? Those are just two examples of situations that would make one uncomfortable who is struggling with the transition from war to home.

I've learned that I need to inhale the moment and take time to digest the situation before making decisions. I've learned that I need to enjoy life and do exactly what I feel called to do and not allow fear to control me.

It has been said that post-traumatic stress disorder, or PTSD, is overdiagnosed, underdiagnosed, and misdiagnosed. Wow ... what a hot mess, yet so very true. The world has never dealt with, nor done too much to try to understand the trauma that comes with service. Unfortunately, it is our veterans who suffer, along with their friends and family, and sometimes complete strangers suffer.

We can waste our time misjudging the situation or what is going on. We need to be vigilant and not complacent. We need to identify the individuals who need us. We need to ask questions and listen. We need to care more!

Twenty-two veterans take their lives daily. Now if that doesn't shake your soul, I'm not sure you have a pulse. We live in a world where we are trained and shaped to be so darn busy and concerned about ourselves that we miss so much. We are complacent to street signs, finishing text messages, emails, verbal conversations in person or on the phone, and reading and understanding body language. Of course, we fail to see the signs from a struggling veteran or anyone else in our lives who might need support and strength in a time of desperate need. Being more proactive rather than reactive needs to be a serious priority.

So how do we prevent this from happening? What do we look for in servicemen and women, or non-service members suffering with the same issues? How can you identify this in yourself if you are the one struggling?

The book of James says, "Celebrate the hard times, for it is the hard times that bring about more strength and perseverance." Celebrate. Does that sound challenging? Sure, but what is the alternative? Well, you could wallow in your sorrows. You can let the hard times dig up those negative feelings, sucking your energy and positivity from you, leaving you feeling insecure, lost, and possibly hopeless. It is not hopeless. What is hopeless is getting stuck in that place in life where you find no fault in yourself for your lack of change or growth. Take accountability, acknowledge it, and move on by working on it one day at a time, one step at a time. Yes, it is easier said than done, but not celebrating the hard times sounds way harder.

"Struggle is useful, and life is life's best teacher." Great insight from Ken Falke and Josh Goldberg, in *Struggle Well: Thriving in the Aftermath of Trauma*. In their book, they teach about the process of post-traumatic growth. We learn from struggle. Bad things happen, and they are inevitable. Trauma can be devastating to your core beliefs about the world. Falke and Goldberg go on to discuss how you can accept the struggle and take the opportunity to look deep within yourself, or you can fight the struggle.

Falke and Goldberg also explain that struggle can bring profound gifts. They describe the process of growth and the pinnacle of success not as the point when you have "made it in life," experiencing a great deal of success, but rather, the pinnacle is when you come back down that mountain of struggle and personal growth to help someone else.

I am not perfect. Ryan is not perfect. We continue through our post-traumatic growth, and it will probably always be a part of our lives. Healing is not an easy process. Worse, realizing that you need some type of healing or release to feel free can be the hardest step. Who wants to acknowledge the things in their life that hinder them or cause the biggest internal, possibly external, challenge in your life? That can certainly be hard for someone to grasp, understand, and plan how to grow from it. I now have a stronger appreciation for life and the things that have happened, even the things that broke me down at the time. I can now say those things happened for a reason.

What is it that you struggle with in life? What is it that is weighing you down or sucking your energy from your life? Identify it, acknowledge your role in it, and don't lie to yourself. With honesty and transparency, more growth can flourish because you know there is room for improvement. Inhale life's pleasures and challenges with a positive mind and resilience. You are a beast. You are stronger than you know. Celebrate the struggle!

REFERENCES

Falke, Ken, and Josh Goldberg. *Struggle Well: Thriving in the Aftermath of Trauma.* Lioncrest Publishing, 2018.

ABOUT THE AUTHOR

Jennifer Hobbs is an Army Veteran whose compassion and humor reaches far and wide through her drive to connect with and support others. She has dedicated over a decade teaching in the education industry and serving Veteran nonprofit organizations. Jennifer is empowered by the personal growth that comes with struggle, and she inspires others how to embrace their journeys as well. When she's not teaching and immersed in her love of writing, she's spending time with her Veteran husband, three kids, and two dogs.

www.thejenniferhobbs.com